FATAMORGANA

a memoir • a corporate takedown • a manifesto

SARAH MAJDOV

This book is based on the author's lived experiences, observations, and interpretations. Names, roles, and details have been changed or blurred where necessary. All institutions are real; references reflect the author's perspective. Some memories are sharper than others. No proprietary information is disclosed. All views expressed are personal. If you think you see yourself in these pages—consider it a mirror, not a spotlight.

For the people still doing real work.
And for those who search for it.

NOTE TO THE READER

This book starts as a memoir.
Then it reads like a corporate takedown.
Then it shifts into a manifesto.

It's a vertigo kind of thing.
And it's ambitious.
Can a book be both ambitious and well-structured?
Maybe.
But I picked ambition.

It's not self-help.
It's something closer to collective help—or at least collective clarity.

It's a reckoning.
A personal one, mostly. But not just mine.

If something feels unfamiliar, it probably means we've lived in different worlds.
You get to decide if that's good or bad.
If you're willing to mind the gap,
Step on.

This book won't dumb things down.
It assumes you're sharp. Or curious. Or at least willing to fake it now
and then.

You'll find fragments of a few disciplines—
There's technology—you can't escape it.
There's philosophy.
Human psychology.
A few Balkan references that might sound foreign.

If you like foreign—great.

If not—¯_(ツ)_/¯

Mostly, it's a mirror.
Held up to the system.
And to me.
And maybe even to you.
But most certainly to us.

CONTENTS

THE QUIET REIGN

THE EMPIRE HAS NO FACTORY

OFFSHORING AND OTHER POWER PLAYS

THE NEXT GENERATION

FIVE FRIENDS, FIVE UNIVERSES

ARRIVAL AND ACCELERATION

DAY 69

Maybe it was because so many before me had arrived there, but I always imagined New York. Walking the streets like in Sting's song. I would be an alien, a legal alien—not an Englishman, but still walking in New York.

But someone, somewhere stared at a map of the U.S. and thought: *Texas has space. Jobs. She'll do fine there.*

So, I landed at DFW Airport, on a one-way ticket from Serbia.

The heat hit first.

I thought it must be from the jet engines: once we left the airport, it would cool off.

It didn't.

I felt like we'd ascended into another layer of the sky and landed without ever coming back down.

The heat bent the air—everything was real and unreal at once.

Close enough to seem solid—but not quite.

I didn't know it then, but distortions would dominate a good chunk of my life in America.

The heat was just the beginning.

Then the scale hit.

Airport, cars, highways, houses—everything was oversized.

Even the sounds—layered, endless, too many kinds at once.

Nothing moved the way I expected.

Luggage had wheels.

Airport cleaners didn't use brooms and buckets; they steered machines.

A man picked me up in an old red convertible—someone sent by the agency that arranged my relocation. He'd arrived from Bosnia a year earlier.

He dropped the top, cranked the A/C, and blasted ex-YU music: Bijelo Dugme, a song about a guy who lost a girl's number and now calls random strangers, hoping one of them is her.[1]

"It's to help you transition gradually," he said, smiling.

"I'll close the roof once we hit the highway. For now, feel the wind in your hair."

It's like he knew I'd remember this day. Like he'd planned it—the car, the music, the wind in my hair. But the music didn't soften the strangeness. It sharpened it. Maybe that was his intention all along.

We drove off.

He dropped me off at the $400-a-month apartment, prepaid for three months.

Wall-to-wall carpeting—soft enough to sleep on. In Bosnia, rugs got dragged outside and hosed down. *How do I clean something I can't drag?*

My new home was in a quiet suburb on the west side of Fort

---

1. That day, one of their lesser-known songs was playing: *Ala je glupo zaboraviti njen broj*—a 1983 track.

Worth, in a place called White Settlement—a name that didn't strike me as odd until much later.

Quiet—except for the air force jets tearing through the silence. Lockheed Martin was nearby. Every time they roared overhead, I stopped. Braced.

Days earlier, I was in a warzone.

NATO had been bombing Serbia for 78 days.

I arrived in America on the 69th.

I waited for years for my U.S. immigration application to be processed and approved. By the time my passport was finally stamped, Serbia was under attack.

It was my adopted country. Or maybe the one that adopted me.

After the war in Bosnia, it had become my second home.

And now my third home—the U.S.—was bombing my second.

NATO—a superpower in the sky—against Serbia, a small country on the ground, scrambling with aged weaponry, outmatched before the fight even began.

I was too desperate to say no to the stamp. Or maybe I wasn't. Maybe I just didn't have enough courage. Or principles. We were still living in a refugee camp in Serbia. And I was too afraid a bomb might find me.

So I packed. And left.

I flew straight into the arms of the war maker.

It wasn't the first time.

Serbia had helped fan the flames of the Bosnian war years earlier—and I had flown into its arms, too.

Always into the arms of the troublemakers.

I've been luckier with men than with countries.

In Serbia, I lived on a mountain near the broadcast towers NATO often targeted, hoping to disrupt news and media. After the strikes, even though our parents warned us to avoid sites that might still carry traces of uranium, my friends and I snuck into the woods to find them.

Craters were massive—forty feet wide.

But the trees were more haunting than the craters.

Freshly felled, sliced mid-air as if an axe had passed through.

Still green. Still alive.

Interrupted in the middle of living.

I touched them. I don't know why.

I was alive. They would dry out and die.

So random—

where they stood, and where I stood, in that moment in time.

I left Serbia, but my body still braced.

Jets passed, but the concussive strikes never came.

Here in America, there were no roars, no explosions.

Only sky—endless, harmless.

The jets weren't dropping bombs here.

Just training.

Training to drop bombs elsewhere.

FROM WAR TO WORK

Most Americans weren't even following the news. Or maybe it only seemed that way, because in Serbia, all we did was follow the news. A few weeks later, the bombing stopped. Milošević[2] signed the peace agreement. Serbia lost Kosovo—again.

Kosovo had been majority-Serb territory for centuries. Blood was spilled to defend it. But over time, the balance shifted. Some Serbs left. Some had fewer children. The Albanian population grew.

When the ground shifts, and a country has no muscle, it's a coin toss whether the map shifts too.

I didn't know any Albanians, but I knew plenty of Serbs. I could already imagine the conversations back home—between friends, family, neighbors. Everyone blaming someone: America, NATO, Albanians, Serbian politicians—for not anticipating what would happen, for not being smarter.

But even an ocean away, I could feel their ache of losing that land.

Meanwhile, in America, life moved forward quickly. Within days, I had my Social Security card, passed my driving test, and found my first job.

---

2. Slobodan Milošević was the president of the Federal Republic of Yugoslavia—comprising Serbia and Montenegro—during the NATO bombing campaign in 1999.

Everything felt seamless. Efficient.

At work, I met Matthew—a college-educated American whose calm confidence I admired.

One day, while we were talking about the future, Matthew asked me, "What do you want to do?"

"I don't know—I just don't want to be poor again."

He gave me advice that changed everything:

"Study computer science," he said.

"If you can graduate, the chances of landing and keeping a good job are high."

I'd never even used a computer, but I had been a math major in Serbia.

The Serbian Red Cross fed us refugees from Bosnia well enough that we never suffered from malnutrition. It was still an era of canned tuna, canned beans, Spam—fiber, protein, preservatives. No sugar. No carbs.

My body was lean. My mind clear.

I handled differential equations and abstract algebra easily. My mom always says we owe more to the Serbian Red Cross than to the U.S. Maybe she's right. They had less power, fewer resources—but somehow, they pulled us through the deepest chaos.

And so, I followed Matthew's advice. I enrolled in the Computer Science Engineering program at UTA. Threw myself into learning machines—their anatomy, how to make them think fast, how they communicate, how to make them scale.

It wasn't easy, but I worked hard, graduated, and found my way into tech—coding, consulting, traveling—instantly adding a zero to my paycheck.

HAVING IT ALL

A t first, my success felt surreal. I forgot how hard I studied. I forgot the pain of finals. Without that memory, it felt like I hadn't earned it—like I had just arrived, effortlessly.

It was like childbirth: in the moment, I'd think, *This is unbearable—never again.* But, before I knew it, I was doing it all over again. We forget the pain, and with it, sometimes, the cost of what we've gained.

Months and years passed, and I found my footing in a world I never thought I'd enter. By the mid-2000s, I was living out of suitcases. Weekly travel, a fast-paced schedule—I was a globetrotting professional. I moved from one client to another, one airport to the next, logging frequent flyer miles across the world: Dubai, London, Manila, Mumbai.

I constantly compared myself—to my former self, to others who shared a similar fate—and all I saw was progress. There was no rocket emoji back then, but if there had been, it would've been mine.

By the early 2010s, I had shifted into even higher gear. My confidence grew—so did my ego.

A master's degree while working? Done.

A kid while earning my master's and working full-time? Done.

Another kid, fifteen months later—still working, still studying? Done.

I kept going. Never missed a beat.

It was a blur of everything: just enough effort at work, a B+ or A– in class, salary still flowing, school years checked off, kids born between semesters. Eight weeks of maternity leave became time to finish another semester and study for finals. Sleepless nights—whether from small kids or exams—had been the norm. I'd never had so much opportunity before, and I was determined to grab everything I could.

I wanted all of it.

While other women wrote articles wondering *Why Women Still Can't Have It All*, I read them puzzled—because somehow, I did. Career, husband, kids, education, travel, money—even good looks.

I had it all.

THE ILLUSION OF MOVEMENT

NOTHING PEOPLE

Throughout my career, I've occupied what I'd call the "Goldilocks position" in the corporate hierarchy—not too high, not too low, but right in the middle, where I could see everything.

In most companies, HR categorized it as Level 4 or 5—high enough to glimpse strategy, low enough to understand execution. The CEO was Level 1, entry-level positions were Level 9, and I was right in between. I could see two levels up, two levels down, and move laterally across departments—technology, business, sales.

I didn't just stay in one lane. I worked across teams, across industries, across clients. It wasn't just one company I was observing—it was a second, a third, and more.

I racked up miles—not just in the air (though there was plenty of that), but miles of realizations.

Patterns emerged, but I didn't dwell on them. I connected a few dots, never enough to see the bigger picture. I moved quickly from one thing to the next, surviving corporate life instead of making sense of it. You notice something briefly—then life distracts you. Do that long enough, and suddenly five years have slipped by.

But then my kids started kindergarten, and suddenly I had something new. I had time.

Was it the extra space in my day that made me finally notice? Or had the nature of work changed, and I was just now seeing it clearly?

At the beginning, I built systems. They worked. People used them. Maybe I didn't make their jobs easier, or their lives easier—but I made an hour or two of their day easier. I delivered something that helped. I could see the output, the impact—even if it was small, it was something.

But then that kind of work became rare. Or maybe it had started disappearing even earlier, and I just hadn't seen it—because I was anchored to a different time—blinded by my own expectations of what work was supposed to be. Maybe I was still learning, and I mistook learning for doing. There was a lag in perception. I'm just not sure what caused it.

Effort at work started leading nowhere.

More effort—still nowhere.

What I thought was a short-term lull stretched into years. Not a drop. Not a ripple. Not even the smallest wave. I couldn't find anything useful to do at work.

And nobody noticed.

Shouldn't work *do* something? Why wasn't anyone noticing? Why wasn't anything changing?

Maybe they just needed time.

But time passed—and still, nobody noticed.

Or they did—but it made no difference.

I was embedded in enterprise architecture, strategy, engineering teams. But I wasn't moving anything forward. Not technology. Not business. Not strategy. Not even a drop of impact. Nothing at all.

I was a Nothing Person.

And it wasn't just me.

I started asking others about their work. "So what are you working on?"

They'd answer—some confidently, some fumbling. I'd dig deeper. Every conversation followed the same arc: "What? Then what? So what?"

Sometimes work looped back on itself like a recursive function. Sometimes it was a dead-end street. Worst of all—a highway that ends midair.

It never added up to anything.

Everyone was like me. Everyone was a copy of a copy of a copy.

Nothing People.

I don't mean people who are worthless. I mean people who have jobs but produce no tangible value.

It's not a moral judgment. It's a structural one.

(Actually, it's a moral one too. It always was.)

Maybe they didn't know.

Maybe they did—and hid it.

Maybe they didn't care.

NOTHING PEOPLE
WITH FULL COFFERS

The story of the next twenty to thirty years will be—what's it like to have an economy that's maybe two-thirds stagnant?"

That's the question posed by economist Tyler Cowen, at Churchill College, Cambridge, in 2024.

AI, biotech, and green energy keep advancing.

But the rest—wages, job creation, productivity, innovation—stuck.

It's not just a feeling. It's in the statistics. Total factor productivity has looked bad for decades. And the latest numbers are even worse.

Almost fifteen years ago, he wrote *The Great Stagnation*. I read it as soon as it came out.

But stagnation doesn't start the moment someone writes about it—let's say it had already been in place for at least five years by then.

Now, fifteen more years have passed, and two-thirds of the economy is still stagnant. That makes twenty years.

And now, he's projecting another twenty to thirty.

If it stretches fifty years—twenty behind us, thirty ahead—is it really just a business cycle?

Or is it something bigger?

I think what he identified on a macro scale, I experienced on the micro level.

I was trapped in that stagnant two-thirds.

That's why I was a Nothing Person, surrounded by Nothing People.

There's always a larger cosmos that explains our small lives.

Every mass revelation comes with an underlying irony.

The companies I worked for made plenty of money. No matter what happened—COVID, mass layoffs, war in Ukraine, any global crisis—someone would always say:

"Well, our cash coffers look good."

We were Nothing People with full coffers.

We could weather any storm—stagnation, stagflation, shrinkflation, inflation, hyperinflation, recession. You name it.

I worked in companies that belonged to the stagnant two-thirds—doing nothing, with people who did nothing.

And yet, these companies didn't just survive.

They thrived.

The coffers stayed full.

At first, it felt like an anomaly.

But as I moved from company to company—consulting, observing—I realized it wasn't just one company. It was entire industries. Banking, financial services, fintech, consulting—saturated with Nothing People, orbiting the full coffers.

How many Nothing People are there? Hard to say. But we can make assumptions. Agriculture and industry make up about 20% of the U.S. economy—let's assume every worker there is a Something Person. The rest? Services: finance, retail, healthcare, education. And in finance and insurance—the worst offenders—easily 80% of the workforce are Nothing People. But they're everywhere: corporate healthcare, academia, large swaths of tech.

At this scale, for every Something Person, there's a Nothing Person. It's all mushed together. There are no clear borders.

It's like spilled oil on the ocean surface—blotches of Something People, dark blotches of Nothing People.

Some areas are all dark.

And no vessel in sight to clean it up.

I didn't have the language for it then.

I found it only later. The Proximity Economy.

THE SWITCH THAT RUNS THE WORLD

Once upon a time—in the '60s or '70s—some very clever engineers built a masterpiece. Picture an octopus swallowing a computer, its tentacles stretching across the globe, connecting banks, merchants, and cardholders into a single, vast network. Inside, it's constantly at work—AUTH, CLEAR, SETTLE—beating like the heart of global finance.

Massive and energy-hungry, this octopus occupies two enormous data centers in Missouri: one near St. Louis, the other in Kansas City. Its name? The Switch.

This is one of Mastercard's greatest achievements—a system that quietly powers global commerce, largely unseen and vastly underappreciated by the world.

At Mastercard, new employees quickly learn about the Switch. From that moment on, there's no confusion—mention "the Switch," and it's not about flipping lights or trading places. It's the Switch. The backbone of Mastercard. The machine that never stops.

Every time the Switch AUTHs, CLEARs, or SETTLEs, it generates revenue—not just for Mastercard but for every bank tied into its rails.

Spend ten dollars at Starbucks, and while most of it goes to Starbucks, small slices get skimmed off for their bank, your card issuer, and Mastercard—each taking a cut to keep the system humming. Those fees are baked into the price of your latte, paid by every customer who walks in.

Though built on decades-old programming languages like COBOL and C, the Switch remains more efficient than most so-called "disruptive" innovations. It processes transactions in 200–300 milliseconds—far faster, at scale, than the blockchain-based systems dominating today's headlines. It runs on mainframes that remind me of Stonehenge—towering, enduring, awe-inspiring.

If the Switch is that old, why not replace it?

Early in my career as an Enterprise Architect at Mastercard, I used to wonder the same.

Because it still works. Perfectly.

Systems like Mastercard's Switch have been optimized nearly to their limits, handling thousands of transactions per second (TPS) with near-perfect reliability. Any further improvements would offer diminishing returns, brushing up against hard physical limits—like the speed of light.

For comparison, blockchain technologies like Ethereum handle about 15 TPS, and Bitcoin manages only 7 TPS. Blockchain isn't built for high-volume, low-value transactions—it's better for large-value transfers where transparency or trust is critical.

Replacing the Switch isn't a question of how but why—and there's no compelling answer.

And Mastercard isn't alone. Visa has VisaNet. Equifax has Core USIS.

Goldman Sachs, Bank of America, JPMorgan Chase—they all have something.

A core. A beating heart.

Each system goes by a different name. Each one routes, matches, verifies, settles, clears, or scores—sometimes silently, sometimes visibly.

ATMs, credit card networks, insurance claim platforms, interbank transfers, trading systems, loan processing, payroll, tax collection, social security, airline reservations, supply chains, utility billing— you name it.

They all rely on central systems. Some route transactions. Some process records. Some make decisions in milliseconds.

Massive, indispensable, and still running after half a century—or longer. And yet, not many people talk about them.

The world chases AI, blockchain, and BigTech revolutions, but OldTech runs the world. Wrapped in APIs, given sleek interfaces, made to look modern—but beneath the surface, the core remains untouched.

OldTech is bedrock. Immovable. Silent. Unyielding.

Eternal.

Indifferent.

And that makes all the difference.

PROXIMITY ECONOMY

Why Proximity?

Because you have to be close—to some kind of machinery. Switches, algorithms, networks, platforms.

If you're close enough, you're wrapped in the illusion of valuable work.

You work—but not in the way you think.

You signal.

The machinery hums, indifferent to your presence.

Proximity—plus a little signaling—lets you reap the rewards.

We signal just enough activity to keep the illusion alive—that the company is innovating, that progress is happening.

So what holds the Proximity Economy together? Three things:

— *Inherited digital machinery (Switches)*—algorithms, networks, platforms. Old, efficient, self-perpetuating. Inside companies, they call them "legacy systems." Sometimes "core systems." Sometimes just "the core." We like to say they're "the bread and butter." But really, they're more like blinis, crème fraîche, and caviar.

— *Gatekeeping*—hierarchy and rewards. The closer you are to the machinery, the bigger the cut.

— *Innovation signaling*—like virtue signaling, but for progress. It's not innovation. It just looks like it.

I respect the first.
I endure the second.
I despise the third—but I play along.

Why inherited machinery?
Because the people running the show today didn't build it.
The brilliance came from elsewhere—engineers from decades ago.
Think Nixon era.

And yet, some new kids on the block orbit their machinery now, pretending they're the ones building the future.

What's left isn't innovation. It's maintenance. A few small, incremental tweaks—just enough to keep the illusion of progress alive.

Meanwhile, the volume of transactions keeps growing. With every swipe, every tap, every deposit, every withdrawal—some intentional, some just forgotten subscriptions—the revenue grows. Even if nothing else does.

Like any broken system, the Proximity Economy should collapse under its own contradictions.

But it doesn't. It adapts—through messaging, signaling, and shared delusion.

It's a barren landscape.

Walking through it feels like stepping into a Dalí dreamscape—cracked earth, tumbleweeds, the distant hum of machinery.

Surreal. Mechanical. Stagnant.

The Proximity Economy is a *Fatamorgana*.[3]

You don't hear that word in America—but in the Balkans, and in other nations too, we know it. Sometimes it's two words. But in the Balkans, it's one.

Fatamorgana means a mirage—seen on land, at sea, in deserts, in the polar regions.

Ships floating in the sky. Islands appearing, then vanishing.

Stacked, distorted images that trick the eye.

But we—the Balkan people—use *Fatamorgana* beyond the literal.

We use it in everyday conversation—it signals more than illusion.

It means false promises. Empty pursuits.

This is the Proximity Economy.

You think you're seeing innovation—people working on valuable, meaningful, real things.

But it's just innovation signaling.

False promises. Empty pursuits.

It takes time to really look—until the mirage fades.

And once you see it, you can't unsee it.

---

3. *Fatamorgana* is a type of superior mirage—where an image appears above the real object due to a temperature inversion. Common over oceans, deserts, and ice, it happens when light bends between warm and cold air layers, creating illusions that look real but aren't. Americans don't really have a word for this. They say 'mirage,' but it doesn't carry the same weight.

INSIDE THE
HIERARCHY

THE MACHINERY
OF HIERARCHY

ome call us knowledge workers. Others call us the laptop class. In academic circles, they call us symbolic capitalists. I prefer algorithmic aristocrats—a term that captures both our proximity to inherited digital machinery and the privileges that come with it. But that proximity also dictates hierarchy—who moves up, who stays put, who is quietly pushed aside.

Hierarchy distorts interactions. It forces us to perform, even as leadership urges us to "bring our whole self to work." A catch-22.

I often wonder—do we even need hierarchy? Most of us are signaling anyway, so what's the point? But other times, I see its utility. A manager's existence signals there's work—and shields me from having to signal for myself.

It's not just protection; it's a practical shield. It makes my own work—or lack of it—feel less exposed. But hierarchy isn't only a shield. It's also a web of interdependence. My manager depends on me as much as I depend on them.

Every February, the Chief Technology Officer would present to Mastercard's Board of Directors. His board material would trickle down to my manager, then to me.

"Can you sprinkle in some technical magic for this section? It's the technology strategy part. You write well—make it sound insightful. It's your opportunity to shine."

The goal wasn't the work itself. It was to convince higher-ups I was an expert worth keeping. That, in turn, validated my manager's value. And it gave the Board the illusion that we were innovating, or staying competitive—or whatever the goal was supposed to be.

We all carried insecurities. No kidding—we were Nothing People with degrees.

But the managers always seemed the most insecure. Their personal anxieties collided with a competitive, optics-driven workplace. Whenever there was some kind of manufactured urgency—perceived risk, high visibility, or a visit from a big boss at headquarters—they flailed like fish on dry land.

Maybe because they had farther to fall. I had a working husband—my risk tolerance was bigger. But some of them were heads of household, with a mortgage, kids in college, hair thinning, waists expanding, a shrinking sense of purpose—all held together by a job where outcomes felt increasingly arbitrary.

One kept a few books in his cubicle: *The Ride of a Lifetime* by Disney's chief bragger, and a couple on cloud security—one to signal leadership, the other technical chops. When he talked about his career, he'd always say, "I was a database programmer." That's how they signal they're worthy. They are legit. A little struggle and smarts a day keeps the doubt away.

Another former executive left Mastercard before I did but started writing a blog. Even outside the workplace, in his own home, he's still signaling. Still trapped in the corporate mindset, unable to shake its grip. His latest post on LinkedIn included lines like, "My work was rewarding and provided opportunities for growth, status, prestige, and visibility."

Status. Prestige. Visibility.

Shouldn't we be a little embarrassed to parade those values around? Another manager I worked with often declared, "I'm not afraid to roll up my sleeves." Roll them up for what, exactly? What does *rolling up your sleeves* even mean in this line of work?

Over time, the Proximity Economy selected the worst Nothing People—those closest to the inherited machinery are the least wholesome, the worst kind of suck-ups to be entrusted with power.

Many are corrupt. Some are delusional. A few are both—intoxicated by their long winning streaks and the safety of their position.

In Bosnia, we have a word for them: *uhljebi*. Americans won't fully appreciate it, but it's a word Bosnians reserve mostly for government bureaucrats who never relinquish their positions. It's so precise that whoever coined it was a genius. It literally means "*embedded in bread*". Bread surrounds you—cushioning, sustaining. You don't earn it; you simply munch whenever you like.

And I can't decide who is more pitiful—the leadership, the managers, or the workers beneath them, so eager to please, so quick to submit. We avoided the head of the table. You stay away—because it doesn't take much to become the meddlesome priest.[4]

The way we forced those submissive grins whenever a leader cracked a joke in a meeting—like monkeys baring their teeth to a dominant alpha.

---

4. A reference to Thomas Becket, the Archbishop of Canterbury murdered in 1170 after King Henry II allegedly exclaimed, "Will no one rid me of this meddlesome priest?"

We grinned and nodded—on autopilot.

A split second later, you catch yourself and cringe.

Maybe places with real work have less of this dynamic.

I wouldn't know.

When most employees don't have anything to do, managers have even less.

No real work means no real autonomy—no debate, no direction. Just the hollow rhythm of compliance.

Quiet quitting—doing just enough, long before the media gave it a name—was already the norm.

"What's it called again?"

"Quiet quitting."

"Can you believe it?"

"Yep. Weird."

"Anyway, what's on the agenda today?"

THE ALGORITHMIC ARISTOCRACY

Titles multiplied, and hierarchies deepened—analyst, consultant, director—each split into junior, senior, principal. Then the VPs: VP, SVP, EVP. Above them, the chiefs—first the old guard: executive, financial. Then the new wave: data, diversity, sustainability. And at the top, the board.

But there were hidden hierarchies too.

An invisible crew cleaned the floors and bathrooms, maintained the campus grounds. They worked as janitors and cooks in the corporate cafeteria. But the invisible crew was outsourced—for cost-cutting, liability dodging, and to preserve the corporate image. Hiring them directly would mean acknowledging their presence—too disruptive to the "core business." It was a system built on invisibility: the corporations that hired them never had to see them, and the corporations that used their services never had to think about them. A win-win.

Maintenance workers kept the Switch alive. They were mostly men with expertise in electronic, mechanical, and electrical systems. Data center technicians, network engineers, maintenance techs—the ones I'd see pushing carts through the hallways, loaded with equipment, cables, laptops needing repair, network testers, servers. Their offices were in basements with fluorescent lighting and no windows. They spent their days updating configurations, replacing hardware, fixing bugs. They oiled the engine—not just of the Switch, but of the whole company.

They never appeared in town halls. No "talent spotlights," no feature stories on the corporate intranet. Maybe because they had actual jobs—jobs that provided tangible value and immediate purpose. And maybe because many didn't have four-year college degrees. Just training. A certificate. Competence. I'd guess no more than one in ten employees typically fell into this category.

Administrators were a group primarily focused on keeping the human side of the machine running—project managers, compliance officers, HR professionals, communications teams, marketers, franchise managers. They handled employee and customer onboarding and offboarding, orientation sessions, compliance training, process management, internal branding, newsletters, town halls. Their work was sprawling, often pulled from thin air. Their rewards were limited—average salaries under $100K—and opportunities to ascend beyond administration, impossible.

Expansion Operators focused on connecting new customers—banks, governments, and tech players—to the Switch. They didn't create anything new; they simply expanded the system's reach. Their work wasn't groundbreaking. It revolved around forms—lots of forms that customers had to fill out. They were always trying, somewhat optimistically, to automate parts of the onboarding process. But automation mostly added cost and complexity. The scale wasn't there—customers were businesses, not individuals, and each had unique requirements. Their salaries hovered just above administrators'—steady but modest. Influence remained superficial.

The rest of the hierarchy was made up of Algorithmic Aristocrats, divided into three subgroups: System Gatekeepers, Innovation Signalers, and Noise Creators.

System Gatekeepers consisted of the Executive and Senior Vice Presidents, along with the C-suite, making up roughly 1% of the workforce. While they performed oversight functions—strategic control, managing acquisitions, and maintaining operational efficiency—much of their work served to perpetuate the system's inefficiencies. They were the gatekeepers of the Switch, its rewards, and, ultimately, the status quo.

Innovation Signalers and Noise Creators were the largest group, constituting roughly 70-80% of the workforce. They specialized in rebranding and repackaging core functionalities of the Switch as "value-added services" to create new balance sheet categories and project an image of "innovation."

I was part of this group. My official titles were System Architect, Enterprise Architect, Core Strategy Architect. My team and I churned out diagrams, projects, processes, and ideas—none of it real work. We needed a philosophy to justify our existence. Ours was *reuse*.

We pitched it as strategic—reuse what other teams had created, work across silos, don't reinvent the wheel. It was signaling how we were supposedly thinking about efficiency.

We reused what didn't exist, on behalf of a need that wasn't real, to solve a problem no one had.

Most of our deliverables—Visio Diagrams, PowerPoint decks—ended up in Confluence graveyards: documents, reports, and plans neatly filed away, untouched, irrelevant, forgotten.

When I think of Innovation Signalers and Noise Creators, I think of gusle players. My grandparents listened to it—a Balkan single-stringed instrument for epic storytelling: grating, abrasive, no melody.

Its only purpose was to demand attention, to fill the air with importance.

But in the end, it was just noise.

THE ILLUSION
OF INNOVATION

THE ART OF SIGNALING

I once heard a leader at Mastercard try to reassure employees: "Sometimes you might be working too far from the customer to see the real impact—but trust that you are making one." That's the blur we're trained to accept—just enough illusion to keep us engaged.
How does corporate signaling actually work?

Patent Filings
Patent filings are subtler—but more devious.
You'd think a company filing patents is doing something real. But no. Usually, it's the opposite. The more patents filed, the bigger the bullshit.
Take one example: Mastercard was granted a patent titled "Method and system for integrating blockchain-based systems with existing payment networks." Like many corporate tech patents, it wrapped old rails in new vocabulary—and got approved anyway.
Sounds groundbreaking, right? Blockchain! Cutting-edge innovation!
It's not. Their core systems—the legacy rails—are centralized, built for speed, efficiency, and control. Blockchain is decentralized, built for transparency and distributed trust. They don't merge; they clash. Not just teleologically, but philosophically. A blockchain system wants

41

everyone to see the ledger. Legacy payments want *no one* to see it. Visa and Mastercard are like Cinderella's stepsisters, jamming their rails into something never meant to fit.

Automation and Abstraction

Over the past twenty years, technology has moved through phases—virtualization, then cloud computing, then containers, and now Kubernetes. Billions have been invested in these. Each step added more automation, but also more layers of abstraction.

These shifts look transformative, but they mostly optimize what already exists.

What would the world look like without them? If you were alive in 2000, you already know. It wouldn't be all that different from 2025.

Repackaging, Repurposing, Rebranding

It's just the old, repackaged as new. Labels like add-ons, value-added services, or new form factors project innovation, often showing up on balance sheets as fresh revenue streams. Value-added services, for example, frequently appear as distinct offerings but are often just peeled from core services of OldTech—repackaged, remarketed, and resold as something new.

True innovation is rare.

To fill the gap, companies leaned into reinvention instead. Amazon signaled this shift with the name of its largest conference: re:Invent. Reinvention has overtaken invention.

As Mark Twain once pointed out: "We simply take a lot of old ideas and put them into a sort of mental kaleidoscope."

That's what we did.

In novels, it might be art—a fresh take on an old theme.

But in corporations, it's not innocent. It's justification. They repackage just enough to make it look necessary. It's manipulation, really.

Fraud Prevention as Signaling

Fear is easy to sell. And with little else to do, vigilance gets exaggerated. The industry justifies itself by building ever-higher cyberwalls, deploying smarter AI, and assigning teams to chase edge cases— things that happen once in a million transactions.

The spending is staggering.

Regulatory Compliance as Signaling

It's no longer just about following rules—it's about proving, endlessly, that the rules are being followed. Entire meetings revolve around documentation gaps, risk assessments, and the ever-present threat of fines. "We need to ensure compliance—we risk being audited," someone says, triggering a chain reaction of concern.

And when consumer data is inevitably compromised? You get a letter. Maybe a class-action lawsuit follows. But most people get nothing. And nothing really changes.

Internal Innovation Signaling

Carefully curated "all-hands meetings" and "fireside chats" are a prime example—complete with music, dynamic lighting, polished slides, and rehearsed messaging. These events mimic the energy of a political rally, designed to foster a sense of unity and purpose among employees. At some point, someone inevitably takes the stage and drops the phrase, "Our culture of innovation is strong".

Physical space alterations—like installing solar panels over parking lots—get loudly advertised across the company. When digital innovation isn't possible, they repurpose the physical. Every phase of the solar carport was celebrated in company-wide emails: *"Parking Lot A completed!" "Phase 2 underway!"*

Even the future gets staged. The "futurists" speak in abstractions, offering no insight, no strategy. We'd log onto a Zoom call, where a carefully curated bookshelf loomed behind them—signaling authority. In reality, they're just recycling a handful of trend articles, repackaging the obvious as prophecy.

There were others. Like Mastercard's beloved corporate adage: *"We are doing well by doing good."*

Isn't that corruption? Not just the traditional kind—their business of extraction—but a corruption of spirit. A collective self-deception.

The former CEO coined the phrase. He was later nominated by Biden to lead the World Bank Group. It's irony, really. He ran the company that extracted from the world. Then he was asked to save it.

Front vs. Back Dynamics

Innovation often appears on the front end—the customer-facing side—masking the stagnation underneath. Take Whole Foods. I once paid with a card, then with my phone, and now I can scan my palm. It feels like progress. Like banking is evolving.

But it's not. These changes come from payment processors and retailers—not from any real shift in financial infrastructure. The same legacy rails still carry the transactions. Same plumbing, new faucet.

We'll probably keep innovating at the surface a little longer. But even there, we're hitting a ceiling. The low-hanging fruit is gone.

Maybe Elon Musk's Neuralink will offer to put a chip in our brains—and we'll check out just by thinking.

Acquisitions and Partnerships

It was about neutralization—not growth.

At best, the startup is absorbed—its culture diluted, its momentum lost.

At worst, its products are shelved, its threat eliminated.

The Power of Sound

Mastercard spent millions commissioning a signature chime—a few notes played when you swipe your card. Internal emails were sent. Well done, Mastercard marketing team! Sound is the new frontier.

Another layer that signals forward momentum. Another way for the chief marketing officer to justify his job. Another way to get backstage with Lady Gaga and post about it on LinkedIn.

ChatGPT and other LLMs

Now even the pretending gets outsourced.

There is even more signaling now. Language models churn out work. People think they've hacked the system.

I almost feel bad for the machine. It reads what we do. It watches our signaling, our hollow gestures of productivity.

And what does it think?

These humans—they aren't working. They're simulating work. They're not running the system. The system is running them.

THE ROCKET CAN'T LAUNCH

think *The Pervert's Guide to Cinema*, a film featuring Slovenian philosopher Slavoj Žižek, helped me see it. I'm not 100 percent sure, but I think it rewired how I read patterns. If you've seen it, you know—you never see movies the same way again.

Žižek teaches you to look past the surface—to notice symbols, patterns, absences. His theory was like a virus, implanted in me. It spread—from film to work to LinkedIn posts to the creeping realization that I, and so many others, are Nothing People.

There were moments when I thought the mirage would finally shatter.

This is it. This will snowball.

This will be the thing that forces people to see the truth.

Graeber[5] exposed the absurdity of bullshit jobs.

Cowen[6] diagnosed two-thirds stagnation.

Musk fired 80% of Twitter—and it kept running.

---

5. Anthropologist David Graeber categorized these roles as flunkies, duct tapers, or box tickers, in his book *Bullshit Jobs*. He argued that over half—yes, you read that right, half—of the work people do is pointless, maybe even destructive. This problem becomes even more insidious when tied to a work ethic that equates self-worth with productivity.

6. Tyler Cowen, in *The Great Stagnation*, argued that much of the U.S. economy—roughly two-thirds—has seen little real innovation or productivity growth since the 1970s

COVID proved how little some jobs mattered.

MAGA[7] fractured over Indian tech labor.

Al-Gharbi[8] laid bare the dominance of the symbolic economy.

And yet—the mirage persists.

The Proximity Economy has its own tensions.

In the Real Economy, workers push back—strikes, unions, collective bargaining.

In the Proximity Economy, the fights are different.

Some disengage quietly. (Quiet quitting, remote work debates—do we even need offices?)

Some chase meaning through ESG initiatives or employer-sponsored volunteer days—claim the day, skip the volunteering, check the box.

Some turn on each other. (Gen Z vs. Boomers, tech bros vs. DEI hires, real engineers vs. slide deck people.)

In the Real Economy, Chinese manufacturing eats away at America's.

In the Proximity Economy, we bite at each other over vibes and perceived relevance. Veterans hiring, women, Muslims, Black, LGBTQ+, neurodiverse—each group fighting for a place in the illusion.

The Real Economy fights for wages, rights, and protections.

The Proximity Economy fights over identity, legitimacy, and meaning.

And yet we stay—working, signaling, waiting.

How do we fill time?

---

7. Tensions within MAGA movements surfaced around the outsourcing of tech jobs and the use of Indian labor—both offshore and via U.S. visa programs. But the outrage didn't translate into a deeper look at what those jobs were actually about—or whether they produced anything real.

8. Musa al-Gharbi is a sociologist who writes about elite signaling, institutional decline, and the rise of a symbolic economy that thrives on appearance rather than substance.

I typed. I produced. I presented. I filled the gaps.

Decks, process flows, white papers, AI-powered dashboards.

KPIs, SLAs, SOPs, SOWs, OKRs, MBOs.

GAO, TOGAF, FEAF.

What's my ETA, ETD, ETC? It's EOD, EOW, EOY, TBD. ASAP.

Golden copies, silver copies, bronze copies.

Blacklists, whitelists, safelists, watchlists.

Green status, red status, yellow status, amber alerts, severity levels.

Frameworks. Methodologies. Paradigms. Synergies.

Inputs. Outputs. Outcomes. Alignment.

And all that work created more work.

Someone had to read it, respond to it, revise it, reframe it.

Meetings to explain it.

Emails to clarify it.

Follow-ups to defend it.

What's the executive going to think? Hot, warm, cold?

You learn to anticipate moods. The unwritten rules. The feedback loops. The whispered advice.

The best days? TGIF.

The very best? An OOO reply.

The worst? Mondays after OOO expired. More noise. More clutter. More junk.

It's like Kessler Syndrome—[9]space debris colliding, fragmenting, colliding again, until low Earth orbit is nothing but an impenetrable minefield of junk.

Clutter in the code. Clutter in the inbox. Clutter in the mind.

---

9. Kessler Syndrome: A chain reaction of space debris collisions that creates so much orbital junk, space becomes inaccessible. Proposed by NASA scientist Donald Kessler.

We filled everything to capacity, tricking ourselves into thinking it mattered.

I didn't remove inefficiencies; I multiplied them.

And it wasn't just harmless bloat.

There's a cost to clutter—beyond the obvious. Beyond the fact that I was paid to create it. Beyond the laptop draining power, the commute burning gas, the hours that could've gone to something useful.

Beyond all that—there's the chance that this very clutter we produce is preventing something real.

A breakthrough.

The rocket can't launch.

Not because of gravity.

Not because of physics.

Because of clutter.

All the people—smart, capable people—trapped in this cycle of waste and redundancy.

The engineers maintaining internal software that didn't need to exist.

The analysts compiling reports that no one reads.

The consultants designing frameworks that will be forgotten in six months.

The architects designing standards and policies that no one follows—but everyone pretends to.

Imagine if all that brainpower—if all those resources—were directed toward something else.

Even if we spent all day staring at a single Picasso in a museum.

It would be more worthwhile.

At least it would be real.

THREE WOMEN,
THREE ERAS
OF WORK

MY MOM → WORK AS SURVIVAL

My mom's jobs were about survival. Mine? Mostly signaling. As for my daughters—I don't know what's waiting for them. The world of work is changing too fast to predict.

I imagine some future generation will study our era—not for its innovation, but for its dense concentration of social and economic change.

One of my earliest memories—maybe *the* earliest—is of my mom refusing to eat vegetables from our garden. Chernobyl had just happened, and she was pregnant with my youngest sister. I was six. People warned that radiation could travel through wind and rain. Ukraine was far from Bosnia—but not far enough. Who knew what was safe? A month later, my sister was born—a healthy baby.

While Bosnia was still part of Yugoslavia, my mom worked in a weapons factory in Bugojno—the town where I was born—making igniters for *nagazne mine* (anti-tank mines).

A few lost a hand. Some lost more. Some died.

She saw explosions. Blood. Chaos. When incidents happened, she picked up smoking—though she never inhaled. She slept during the day. I don't know what she did at night. It would last a few days, and then she'd stop smoking, and just like that—she was back. The normal mom.

Then the war happened. We escaped it and lived as refugees in Serbia. My mom was in her early thirties and made a living selling cigarettes. When the U.S. and its allies imposed harsh sanctions on Serbia for its role in the Bosnian War, everyday life collapsed. Sanctions created shortages. And shortages created new economies. Enterprising—or desperate—people found ways to buy scarce staples like cigarettes or gasoline cheaply in one place and resell them elsewhere. My mom chose cigarettes. Risky, yes—but still safer than making land mines.

My uncle called us mafia when he visited the refugee camp up in the hills of Fruška Gora,[10] where we were stationed. He'd walk in the door, grin, and say, *Oh, đe si mafija?*[11] — delivering the fruit my mom had ordered from the *pijaca* in Novi Sad.

He was doing the same thing—running whiskey across the border in his blue Yugo, paying off border patrol with a bottle of Jack Daniels.

With cigarette dealing, the worst that could happen was dealing with the police—a force of underpaid men mom usually knew how to negotiate with.

She traveled by train from Belgrade to Podgorica, Montenegro, smuggling cigarettes across the border. She would pack them into her luggage, sit back in her seat, and put on her best clothes and makeup to avoid suspicion. Sometimes, I traveled with her.

---

10. A beautiful national park in the Vojvodina region of Serbia.

11. *Oh, đe si mafija?* is a casual greeting, roughly: "What's up, mafia?". It's not literal—it's affectionate.

Once, I was with her when we got caught. Border patrol pulled us off the train and held us at a station for a day.

I remember napping on a police station bench while my mom negotiated. As refugees, we didn't have Serbian documents—just papers that marked us as displaced. She had invested 500 Deutsche Marks—a fortune for us—into the batch of cigarettes we were smuggling. After some back and forth, the officers let us go, confiscating only two cartons "to teach us a lesson."

But most of the time, she made it back to our spot on Iriški Venac without any problems. It was a busy intersection in Fruška Gora, where we lived in an old 4,000-square-foot building—about the size of a big American house—housing around forty refugees. Modest, but surrounded by forest and the cleanest air. Who gets to live in a national park? Only the lucky ones.

There was a gas station a short walk from our hotel.

During the day, she sat at the intersection under the hot sun, selling cigarettes illegally.

Afterward, she'd sit at a sewing machine and fix the clothes the Red Cross had brought—altering them to fit my sisters and me.

Eventually, she got an umbrella and even made makeshift signs out of cigarette boxes—advertising Lucky Strike and Marlboro.

She later expanded, selling cans of soda like Fanta and Coke that she bought wholesale in Novi Sad and resold for a small profit. The local police knew our situation—they knew she was a refugee with three kids to feed—so they let her operate, turning a blind eye to the "illegality" of it all.

But my mom's job was more than selling cigarettes. She was also saving lives—and cars.

The intersection at Venac was dangerous; it had a fork where drivers often missed the signs—because at the time there was only a small sign on a side. Now they have a big one over the top.

Drivers would turn the wrong way onto a one-way mountain road, against the flow of traffic.

And it was downhill and winding—crashes inevitable.

My mom, sat there day after day, became a sort of guardian. She'd spot the mistakes, jump up, and wave her arms, yelling at drivers to turn back before it was too late. I watched this play out more times than I can count.

Some drivers yelled, asking why she was screaming.

Mom would shout, "You're going the wrong way!"

They'd turn, realize what could've happened, make a U-turn, and come back to awkwardly apologize. Sometimes others joined in the screaming—an employee from the gas station, a passenger stepping off a bus.

This went on for months—until a local roadside assistance driver realized his business was slowing down. Fewer wrecks meant fewer cars to tow off the mountain road. He confronted my mom, warning her to stop "interfering" with his income. She ignored him. Eventually, he called the police, accusing her of being some big-shot cigarette smuggler with stockpiles hidden at our refugee camp—the real mafia. Several police officers showed up in our tiny room. They found nothing, but warned her to stop selling at the intersection—or else...

That was the end of her job.

Soon after, I left for America and started sending her money. She didn't have to hustle anymore.

Then I heard about him again—years later. Tragically, he lost his wife and young son in Belgrade—they were struck by a car as they tried to cross the road. I don't bring this up to make a point. It's just what happened.

Mom is in her sixties and lives in America now. She became a U.S. citizen in 2004 through the family reunification program—made possible after I became a U.S. citizen. She arrived at forty-five, learned English, completed pharmacy technician training, and now works at CVS in Mount Prospect, IL—counting medications and shipping them to people who need them.

She rarely makes mistakes. A pharmacist friend once told her, "If you leave, we'll have to double-check everything."

But now the systems are automated—Eyecon machines count the medications, QR codes cross-check the prescriptions—it's hard to make a mistake anyway.

It's hard on her feet, but she loves it. She says she'd be bored if she quit.

I never told her about my job. Maybe one day she'll read about it here.

If I tried to tell her, she'd probably brush it off—say it's an imaginary problem.

But maybe, reading it like this, she'll see it differently.

I imagine she'll ask me, "Why in the world did you do it for that long?"

"Nije ti bilo o glavu.[12]"

---

12. It wasn't life or death. That's what she'd mean.

ME → WORK AS SIGNALING

nlike my mom's, my jobs were not about survival. She worked for needs—food, school shoes. I worked for... I don't even know how to categorize it. Still needs, but also conveniences. Then ultimate convenience. Ultra comfort. Anything that saved me time. And over time, everything just got more expensive.

My titles sounded impressive—Enterprise Architect, Director of Market Enablement, Director of Core Strategy. But Mastercard inflated titles to keep employees satisfied on paper. I had no real decision-making power—except, occasionally, to shut down a conversation. And those who did? Their decisions were inconsequential. The initiatives, the strategies, the pivots—they didn't need to exist. All motion, no consequence. A performance of change, not actual change.

At some point, they labeled me a "T-person."

An "I-shaped" person goes deep in a single domain—that's the vertical line.

A "T-shaped" person still goes deep, but also works across—collaborating with other functions, other domains. That's the horizontal line across the top. Just another metaphor. Probably dreamed up at McKinsey, then copied everywhere.

For five years, I earned a generous salary for delivering just enough optics to justify my role—and theirs. These executives steered the ship with calculated moves, while the sea below remained calm, requiring little navigation. Beneath me were senior engineers, consultants, business analysts, and anxious new recruits—wide-eyed, eager, and desperate to climb the corporate ladder.

Every few years, leadership shuffled, and a new tech trend—modularity, cloud integration—would spark another bold initiative: *New Switch, Next Edge, Network of the Future*. Announcements went out, internal web pages went up, stakeholders were mapped.

Even the physical environment transformed: colorful wraps with project names adorned support poles across the open office, while teams clustered into newly designated "collaboration zones."

For a moment, it felt like something transformative was about to begin.

We're going to transform the Switch.

It won't be a monolith—it'll be built on the latest microservices architecture.

But then reality hits.

Someone realizes the core has to stay monolithic.

The projects shrink. The ambition fades.

Sometimes they stall altogether.

A multi-year, multi-million-dollar effort like *Network of the Future*, launched with fanfare in 2017, simply ended one day in 2021.

Eventually, someone catches on: you can't keep promising the future forever. It turns into a hollow slogan. Then comes the standard EVP email: "We are discontinuing the name, but the project is still very much on—we are continuing to push forward."

Leadership can't admit failure.

There's no obituary. Just a quiet rebranding into silence.

After a while, I recognized the pattern: a jolt that felt real, urgent, like it might lead to something—and then, nothing.

Maybe we can prevent the next mass murder? Jolt.

We started digging into payment data, looking for patterns around gun purchases. In payment transaction data, there's a merchant code for every type of store—except gun stores. Weird. We need to fix this.

Payment messages don't show SKU-level data. Even if we know it's a gun store, how do we know it was a gun—and not a fishing rod?

Still, there are available fields. We could add it to the transaction message format.

Aurora. Pulse. Las Vegas.

Mass shootings that made headlines, then slowly faded.

$9,000. $26,000. $94,000.

All in gun purchases. All charged to credit cards in the weeks before.

They're signals—patterns that suggest someone might be cooking something. Mastercard and Visa have enough data to tip someone off. To give law enforcement a reason to look. A chance to intervene—before it happens.

We reached out to other departments.

I go for a run in the park, and my mind races faster than my body.

We'll need to reach out to Visa, talk to their team—this requires both parties.

You start picking up the phone—you can't wait for emails. You work past hours. Interest spreads.

Then an omnipotent executive—the *good idea killer*—shut it down with a single email.

Too controversial. Privacy concerns. Second Amendment. Gun rights groups. Republican state attorneys general won't like it.

And just like that—another one bites the dust.

And just like that—I went back into hibernation.

When I first joined Mastercard, I bought into the story.

I believed we could innovate. Make a difference.

I was labeled a *Talent Employee*—handpicked, high-potential.

They even sent me off-site for a week of company-sponsored acting classes.

To work on my "executive presence."

The lead actor taught us to step onto the stage, feel the ground beneath our feet. She stamped—"This is your grounding. Don't stomp in real life, but feel it. Root yourself. Now command attention."

The irony of being taught how to act for a job built on pretending and signaling didn't hit me until much later.

I recall a moment when a coworker—a fully grown man—broke under pressure while giving a prepared speech. Tears welled up as he stood in front of the rest of us. At the time, it felt awkward. I wasn't sure what to do—look away to give him privacy, or meet his eyes like the lead actor had instructed.

I felt a flicker of relief: at least I wasn't the weakest one in the room.

Now, of course, I see it differently.

We were all someone's children—seeking approval, fearing judgment.

In the second year, my role shifted quietly. Instead of asking, "What can I accomplish today?" I began to ask, "What will look like a productive activity?" What started as an occasional tactic to appear busy eventually became my default approach. Gradually, I learned to recognize the signaling patterns: recycled ideas, hollow pitches, and people joining conversations not to contribute, but to promote themselves.

I became the "idea killer." It wasn't a title I gave myself—it came from a coworker. I corrected him once: "I'm a bad idea killer." I killed bad ideas before they could generate too much noise. Why let the Switch be misinterpreted, debated, or rebranded yet again? But I had my own inertia, too. Maybe I killed a few good ones along the way.

A few days ago, I was killing flies in my house.

Swat, swat, swat.

Then, out of habit, I crushed an innocent ladybug on the window. I froze, staring at it. Innocent, unintended, but gone all the same. Maybe I'd done the same with ideas.

Every February, the bonus hit. I vividly remember sitting in my manager's office during my first year, saying, "I don't feel like I deserve this, but thank you." In the years that followed, I stopped saying that— not because I felt I deserved it, but because I realized nobody did.

That bonus alone was more than the yearly salary of most of my family members—some of whom have college degrees. People who clock in and out of real jobs every day. There's guilt. But it doesn't last long. Maybe an hour or two. What am I going to do? Return the money? Of course not. But in that hour or two, I do think about it. How does the universe explain this?

— Karma: You benefit now, but what goes around comes around.

— Christian God: Whatever one sows, she will also reap. Enjoy purgatory.

— Allah: Whoever intercedes for an evil cause will have a share in the burden.

— The Simulation Hypothesis: That's part of the game. You're
the entertainment.

With all the human ingenuity across history, why does money
still move so arbitrarily?

Every system needs a critical mass of believers to function. And signaling—by its very nature—is secretive. You don't openly talk about
it. I was never sure how many of my coworkers truly saw it for what
it was. Whenever I interacted with someone, I'd wonder: *Do they
know? Are they aware we're just playing the game?*

There was a coworker I thought had to know. He was sharp. He
had to see through it. But then he left, joined another employer, and
started commenting on ex-coworkers' social media posts reminiscing
about the "good times and outcomes" on some past project. I knew
that project. I knew the outcome—gone with the wind. That's when
I realized: he actually didn't know.

It stretches across borders. I've seen it in other countries too—
in offices in Mumbai. Even my tour guide was signaling. The company paid for a driver and a guide to show me the city. She wore a
sari, a red bindi on her forehead. Later, I asked if her kids wore saris
too. She laughed:

"I'm in yoga pants just like you," she said. "The sari's just for show.
For business people."

She was signaling for me. I was signaling for the corporation. The
corporation—for the whole system. Like babushka dolls—we stack
signaling inside signaling until it becomes its own economy.

It got more complicated when I was working under a manager
who didn't see it. They were eager to do things. It's like their parents
read them the Protestant Work Ethic as a bedtime story.

The balancing act was uniquely exhausting: playing along with their sincerity while constantly reminding myself it was all an illusion—just to keep my sanity.

And I often failed at this.

This "talented employee" managed to rack up three PIPs[13] before my career there fizzled out.

Over time, I developed a strategy for surviving the PIPs. I actively resisted the ridiculous—the clear-cut signaling tasks, the completely mindless work my manager would assign. The kind of task they assigned just to feel like they were doing something. Something—anything—to show movement. Or even the normal signaling work, if it involved people I didn't like working with.

My manager would get pissed. A virtual 1:1 meeting would appear on my calendar.

When I sensed something bad coming—the "you don't get to do what you want, you do what I tell you" meeting—I had a rule: no camera.

There was something about not seeing the other person. I got to say what I thought. She got to say what she thought. The filter would drop, and things got raw. I pushed back.

"That's not something I can do. I've never done anything similar. I don't think I have the skills."

"I don't see much need for this. I don't see much value."

"I'm busy with other things."

"I have my butt to scratch." I didn't say that part, but I wish I could.

She would say I was uncooperative. And she was right. I was

---

13. A PIP (Performance Improvement Plan) is, in theory, a tool to help underperformers improve. In practice, it's often a managerial venting mechanism—especially when someone isn't doing enough signaling work to prop up the team's optics.

difficult. But what she was really asking was for me to help maintain the fog. And that demands, at the very least, occasional resistance—and the discomfort that comes with it.

Then her manager would be looped in. Another 1:1—this time, with both of them.

This meeting was different. Camera on.

She'd come in prepared—reading off a laundry list of my supposed offenses, carefully curated, forced politeness. The story neatly constructed, the narrative airtight.

But in that second meeting, I went silent.

I let her finish. Let her pause, waiting for me to resist. I didn't. Poker face. No warmth, no coldness—just blank.

Every manager backs his direct report—that's what makes a "good" manager. So he'd chime in—vague, but ominous:

"These are serious problems."

I'd respond with a single phrase: "I understand."

Their words hung in the air, waiting to be absorbed. Instead, they bounced back in the echo chamber they built. Silence let them hear themselves. And that was the best thing I could do. The power hierarchy was already set—nothing I said would change my position. But I could be silent. At least then, their own words could speak volumes.

They forgot about the happy hour later in the day. They didn't expect me to show up. But I did. And for a moment, they weren't sure how to act. I let them squirm. Then I accepted the drink.

I could tell they felt bad about themselves. Overcompensating, their tone suddenly went soft.

Maybe it was empathy. More likely, they just didn't like seeing themselves that way—like a parent who punishes too harshly, then regrets it minutes later.

It was the best strategy.

But this is only something I got in year three. Year one and two of PIPs are just stress. Stress you carry in your shoulders, your gut, your sleep. The night before, I'd replay the scenarios—anticipating what I'd say, what they might say in return, calculating the best way to retain some agency, some freedom, while still preserving the job. I'd lose sleep. My immune system would weaken. My ability to fight off infections would drop. The stress lingered in my body longer than it should have.

At the end of the year, I'd be placed on a PIP. My bonus would take a slight hit—maybe $10K less than if I had just played along. If I hadn't resisted the nonsense. If I hadn't pushed back.

My husband would say, "$10K? Was it really worth resisting? We could have gone somewhere nice—sun, ocean, guided tours."

For a second, I'd picture it—the trip, the indulgence, the ease of just going along. No stress. No weakened immune system.

Then, just as quickly, I'd rewind—to that 1:1. The quiet satisfaction of not playing along, of withholding the joy she'd get from thinking she was managing, contributing, mattering—that she was a *Something* person.

Why?

When I can hold up a mirror and show her she's a Nothing person.

At least in that moment—while I was holding the mirror—I was doing something. I was a *Something* person.

"It was worth it!"

After a month of busywork disguised as "correction," everything quietly reset. No one followed up. Nothing changed.

Mastercard didn't just stagnate in innovation; it stagnated in firing me.

My tenure had a stubborn permanence. A close friend said: "You're like Nancy Pelosi—they can't get rid of you."

MY DAUGHTER →
WHAT COMES NEXT

'm drying my daughter's hair. She's only twelve, but she's already a connoisseur of a good blow-dry—and I'm proud to match, even surpass, the results she'd get in a salon. As I work, she reminds me she's almost done with her book and asks, didn't I say I'd give her some money for every one she finished? I did. It's my way of hedging against screen time. I'm that parent who pays their kids to read, for better or worse.

She tells me she's saving up.

"For what?" I ask, curious.

"Oh, nothing in particular. I just like saving."

"Well, I'm saving for you," I remind her.

"No, that's for college. I want to save for the things I want to buy… plus, I like having my own money."

She says it with conviction, already thinking about earning, about building something of her own. The individualist mindset has already taken root.

Growing up in a communist society, my parents were almost guaranteed employment—because every company was state-owned. I never asked myself, *What do I want to be when I grow up?* No one asked me either. We were all expected to be workers—part of the system, filling whatever role was needed. My dreams were smaller, but so were my anxieties. I didn't worry about building a future for myself because, in a way, one of the state-owned companies in my city had already mapped it out for me.

My daughter feels the weight of freedom—the open-endedness of her future. And yet, automation looms. Networks expand. The managerial class in BigTech and OldTech tightens its grip.

They don't just enforce the rules—they create them. Not just rulers, but architects of reality. Their logic, their worldview—hardcoded into platforms, embedded in algorithms, shaping work, corporate culture, opportunity, and even thought itself.

Choice exists, but only within their parameters. My generation still carries the inertia of autonomy, of meritocracy—but those are mostly illusions. And we're handing down the same illusion to my daughters' generation, expecting them to run with it, as if it's still real.

But her path feels as preordained as mine was under communism. Maybe even more rigid than mine.

At least the workers in state-owned factories made something real—furniture, building materials, clothes, machinery parts. Even weapons.

I don't think she'll be in the creation industries. Manufacturing keeps shrinking as a share of GDP. As societies grow richer, they consume more services. We're already awash in goods—so saturated that making more feels redundant.

And if we're hit with declining population on top of that, she won't be creating. She'll be servicing. But at the very least, I need to believe she won't be serving fugazi.[14]

I've watched them gravitate toward art. My older daughter pours herself into theater; my younger plays the cello. When they were little—when I was still enchanted with my career—I planned to steer them toward STEM, to encourage them to follow in my footsteps. I taught them multiplication tables at five.

I'm sober now. I don't want to push them into STEM. A hyper-competitive field where men still scramble for relevance in industries automation has already reshaped.

I've been honest with them lately: my job doesn't feel meaningful, even though it pays well. I'm not proud of how I spend my days.

My husband hates when I say this. He thinks it's a burden to them, a risk of killing their ambition.

"They're smart. They'll figure it out," I tell him.

"Maybe they'll be like me—just happy to get a paycheck and not care about a meaningful job," he says. Then, after a pause, he adds, "My employer is taking time away from my health, from my family, from my joy. They need to pay for that."

I almost give him a hug, but then he keeps going.

"Don't forget—when we were in the refugee camp, I was sixteen, working on the plantation picking fruit. Ask your mom—she worked alongside me. We'd get pear juice stuck in our hair, and the bees would attack us until it hardened like glue. I worked in the forest, raking trees. In America, my first job was in a hot factory. Then I moved up—busboy, waiter, software engineer."

---

14. That word from the *Wolf of Wall Street*—fake, made-up, nothing real. A perfect word.

"I want my kids to be able to work—hard jobs, demeaning jobs, bullshit jobs. I don't care, as long as they put food on the table."

I try to imagine my older daughter doing some hard, demeaning, bullshit job just to put food on the table. She's twelve—and still sleeps with her teddies. She has eleven. Each one has a name. Parents, grandparents, friends—we've all showered her with teddies over the years. Recently, she drew an art piece that got noticed by her teachers and was featured in the school exhibit. It was a drawing of her teddies, titled

"Am I Too Old?"

Even if manufacturing does have some kind of renaissance in America—I still can't imagine her doing the kind of job he talks about. When I try, I picture a factory worker in China—a mother, sitting all day at a sewing machine, stitching the teddies that kids like mine cling to.

Does my daughter need eleven teddies? Of course not.

My guess is ten of them—Alan, Elizabeth, Uni, Honey, Blue, Roxy, Baby Bear, Mommy Bear, Daddy Bear, Melody—will end up in a landfill.

Within a few years, maybe less.

We gave gifts on impulse—something to hold, then let go. The lifecycle of a teddy is a chain of impulses. Discarding them will be a sorrowful day for me. Creation leaves a mark—on memory, on landfills, on our sense of what matters.

And that's just their gentle side.

There's also a spoiled side.

The other day, we ordered takeout through a delivery app. The girls forgot to add sauce to the order.

The food arrived, we all sat down to eat—but one of them just sat there, waiting.

I asked, "What are you waiting for?"

She said, "The sauce."

I said, "There is no sauce, honey. Just eat without it."

She replied, "Oh, I placed the order for the sauce. I'll wait."

She had placed a separate order—just for sauce.

I couldn't believe it.

If she can't eat chicken without the right sauce, how are they ever going to be able to do the kind of job he talks about?

I don't tell him that.

They're gentle, a little spoiled—but they also have that spark of human ingenuity.

She wanted me to make her a pistachio cake.

I told her, "We don't have a mixer in this house."

It was in another house.

She went to the garage, grabbed a drill, taped a whisk to it, and started beating eggs.

It worked beautifully.

You need scarcity to see that kind of brilliance.

But real scarcity? That's hard to come by these days.

He lets me spiral for a while. Then he says:

"In poor countries, nobody talks about finding meaning in their work," he continues. "Tell that to someone in Bosnia. Tell that to your mom or dad—they'd never even consider it. The Chinese, Indians, South Americans—none of them worry about it either. That's something rich Westerners discuss over brunch."

He always circles back to pragmatism—Maslow's bottom rung: fear, survival, a full belly.

But it's also aimed at me—because I talk about the illusion, the fakery, the lack of meaning.

I tell him it's all connected.

The same forces that strip my work of meaning are the ones that leave others just getting by. The symbolic class extracts. We invent fictional jobs, lean on reserve currency illusions, shuffle money, inflate assets. And all of it leaves others behind.

Some jobs are shipped overseas. Others, automated away. We lose skills. We lose faith. We lose pride.

Over time, you get a hollowed-out economy still pretending it's the real deal. A leadership trying to bring back factories, as if that alone could restore growth for those left behind.

But the rot is internal. The symbolic class is the Trojan horse—extracting from within.

And still, the labor force believes it can pull itself up by the bootstraps.

America needs new metaphors.

So yes—maybe poor people don't ask whether their jobs are meaningful. But their lack of well-paid jobs and my lack of meaning come from the same place. Two sides of the same hollow economy.

I look at him.

"Are you aware they might grow up to be just like me—sharp, capable, outwardly successful… and swallowed whole by a pretend job."

I glance toward the next room—she is reading. I point.

"Imagine her. Slightly slouched like that—but instead of a book, a laptop in her hands. She'll be in a job that offers no tangible impact.

Eager to contribute, but quietly anxious. Busy fulfilling optics, wondering why she can't find anything meaningful to do."

He doesn't like that image.

"Well then, allow me to tell them exactly what I do—
     So they know what not to become."

THE QUIET REIGN

IN THE SHADOW OF THE SWITCH

There were days when I'd arrive at work—a corporate tech campus—and it felt like stepping into a space that should have been a museum. It was easy to picture: glass walls, open spaces, sleek interiors—polished, almost curated. Not Louvre-level, but not a gimmick like the Museum of Broken Relationships in Zagreb either. I held a quiet reverence for its history, as though the brilliance of the past still lingered in the air.

I'd scan my badge, pass through security, imagining visitors lining up past ticket counters. A short shuttle ride would take them to the data center—the museum's other wing—to admire a vast network of machinery built by minds long gone. Cold galleries, silent but for the hum of servers. Plaques bearing the names of engineers who once shaped entire industries.

At the center, a monolithic structure: *the Switch*. Cordoned off behind a velvet rope. Functional, enduring, frozen in time. A relic for those who value function over form, its presence finally acknowledged by the world it upholds. The employees working around it were its caretakers. Its systems had been running the commerce world for decades, untouched by hype cycles, unfazed by disruptions.

But this wasn't a museum. There were no tickets, no tours—just employees performing innovation in a space where nothing ever truly moved.

The illusion of my work always rested on an old Switch. I had access. I could see them. Touch them. Run the key across when no one was watching.

These machines live in data centers—precise, cold, sterile, almost clinical in their design. It's as if an entire river has been compressed into metal boxes, where information and power flow relentlessly. Rivers are unpredictable. But this one is mission critical, scalable, and fault tolerant. Racks of hardware stand like sentinels. Cables are neatly bundled and color-coded, blinking lights pulsing in a rhythm only they understand.

Standing next to them, there's no sense of inferiority. Their original architects—long retired or six feet under. I never knew them. If I did, maybe there would be a privilege, a burden, in working so close to their creations. But there are no Von Neumanns[15] left to admire— no descendants of his genius to follow. Only the machine remains— indifferent to who comes and who goes.

The hum is omnipresent, a low, droning current that seeps into the body. The electromagnetic fields saturate the air. My mitochondria don't belong in these fields; they vibrate like atoms on the edge of a phase change—agitated, unsettled, displaced from their natural rhythm.

It's a clash between the charge of the oldest biological engine— primordial molecules nearly four billion years old— and the signal emitted by its descendant: the computing machine.

---

15. John von Neumann was a Hungarian-American polymath who made foundational contributions to computer science, mathematics, physics, and economics. He was a key figure in developing early computer architecture—so influential that the basic design of most modern computers is still called the "von Neumann architecture."

Stepping outside, all I want is to take off my shoes, press my feet into the grass, and let the ground reclaim whatever the mechanized monolith has stolen—

some essential charge, some quiet hum of my own.

But the static lingers. Even in open air, I still feel the pulse of the machine. Its rhythm imprints itself onto mine.

But the machine doesn't care. It endures, untouched, while I—while we—struggle to find our place in its shadow.

Technologists in the innovative third of the economy might still be building something tangible—maybe even something that serves a greater good.

But in the stagnating two-thirds, we don't even get to "build fast, fail fast." We just hover in place.

The inherited machine—the old switch—mocked my attempts to transform it. Diagrams, pitches, new ideas—it needed none of it. Nice try. And a wink.

Like countless others, I was just a shadow passing over its surface, leaving no mark.

There was never space—never a chance to shape, improve, or transform a single thing.

IF THEY WERE HONEST

Visa's CEO reported results. The message is always the same—only the numbers change. Below is how Visa would report them if they were fully transparent.

My commentary is in parentheses.

Today, we reported our Q1FY25 results, delivering 10% net revenue growth, 8% GAAP EPS growth, and 14% non-GAAP EPS growth. Visa's strong first-quarter results reflect:

— *Payments volume* (how much money consumers move through our network).

— *Cross-border volume* (our cut from international transactions—mostly extracted from Europe, but also from other markets, plus the fees Americans pay when they use their Visa cards abroad).

— *Processed transaction growth* (more swipes, more revenue).

As we continue through 2025, we remain focused on serving our clients and "innovating" (actually, extracting) across our three growth levers:

— *Consumer payments* (nothing new—this is our Switch, doing what it has done for seventy years).

— *New flows* (growth through acquisitions—buying rather than building, with products often shelved if they threaten card payments).

— *Value-added services* (taking functions that used to be part of the Switch, peeling them off, repackaging them, and selling them back as something new).

Visa's and Mastercard's whole business model is: run a 70-year-old system, absorb threats, and strip the core for parts to resell. *Pure extraction.*

Now, let's look at Mastercard.

Mastercard's CEO posted a LinkedIn status about innovation in payment industry. Same script as always—innovation signaling, vague tech jargon, and fear-based marketing. Here's what they're actually saying:

Universal Keys

"Today, identity authentication is characterized by repetitive logins. In the next ten years, digital identities will resemble universal keys—secured by biometrics, tokenization, and AI-powered security—granting instant access across payments and more."

None of this holds up. Is authentication really "characterized by repetitive logins?" No. Face ID, Touch ID, and saved logins already made authentication seamless.

Biometrics? Already exists.

Tokenization? Already exists.

AI-powered security? That just means automating what's already automated.

And what is "granting instant access across payments and more?" Payments are already instant. What's "and more?" Empty filler.

Wallets to Command Centers

"Digital wallets are popular but limited in functionality. Digital wallets will evolve into proactive assistants that manage finances, travel, health records, subscriptions, and more."

Apple Pay and Google Pay already built digital wallets. The idea that wallets will "manage and be proactive assistants" is absurd.

Finance? Sure, you can see your transactions—just like you always could.

Travel? Boarding passes have been stored in wallets for years. Nothing new.

Health records? Insurance cards have been in wallets forever.

Predictive + Proactive Defense

"AI-powered tools are already identifying fraud in real-time. Adaptive intelligence will enable predictive defenses. And by the end of the decade? Self-healing security systems."

"AI-powered" just means slapping an AI sticker onto existing processes.

"Predictive defenses" is just making fraud detection slightly less reactive.

"Self-healing security systems" nothing but fear-mongering wrapped in a sci-fi buzzword.

BUFFETT'S BET

Picking on billionaires feels like a cheap shot. Especially when they look like a lovable Pixar character. Add a folksy cult of personality, and suddenly it feels like you're punching air.

That billionaire is Warren Buffett.

He thrives in the entrenched two-thirds of the economy. His portfolio is a who's who of financial gatekeepers—American Express, Bank of America, Goldman Sachs, Visa, Mastercard.

Monopolistic corporations that thrive on network effects, killer acquisitions, moats, and inertia.

Yet he never critiques the structural inefficiencies from which he directly profits.

He'll occasionally nod at inequality—but it always comes down to this: the wealthy, like him, should pay more taxes. It's the safest concession he can make—one that pleases critics without ever threatening the system that serves him.

Lately, he's been hoarding cash, offloading Apple, Bank of America, and others.

With two-thirds of the economy stagnating, Buffett's stance makes sense.

As he recently admitted, "nothing looks compelling" enough to invest in.

The system needs men like Buffett—not to build, but to bless it with credibility.

He doesn't run the illusion.

He's like the Orthodox priest at a Serbian *slava*—officiating, legitimizing, giving the illusion its sacred glow.

His company now holds more T-bills than the U.S. Federal Reserve.

We call it investment.

The world calls it what it is: oligarchy.

Bernie Sanders and Alexandria Ocasio-Cortez are out on their *Fighting Oligarchy* tour, trying to revive a tired Democratic Party. It's good. They should.

But it's hard to lift spirits with the same narrow framing. The same tired lines.

They always point to the top 0.01%.

Why not go broader—and deeper?

The real power sits in the collective oligarchy—the executives, managers, symbolic class.

They don't just hoard wealth. They manufacture narratives. Control perceptions. Engineer consent.

Why don't they talk about them?

About inherited digital machinery. About the Proximity Economy.

Beneath the surface, there are Grand Canyon–deep layers of performance and inefficiency.

Is it not visually compelling enough?

Or do they simply lack the language to name them?

Or worse—do they not even see them?

If Buffett and the others extract from above, the leaders of the symbolic class—the VPs, SVPs, EVPs, and C-suite—extract from within.

They operate at a different altitude than billionaires, but it's the same game—extract, wait, preserve, repeat. They're like the Wizard of Oz: projecting the image of visionaries, but really just pulling levers behind a curtain. Not builders. Not leaders. Just operators of inherited digital machinery.

They don't have the hyper-strategic slickness of McKinsey types. What they project is *performative humility*.

They wear jeans on stage. Talk about their families, their pets, or how they got sun-burned doing yard work. The comms department once sent around a video of the CTO demonstrating how to fold an Oru kayak. They project casual relatability.

Strip away the yardwork stories and the 'be safe out there' emails, and what's left is Nothing People in Leadership—holding systemic-level responsibility that history may one day judge with Nuremberg-level moral gravity.

They're Blagojevićs—who never spent a day in jail.

Tony Blairs—for the ideological shape-shifting.

Lindsey Grahams—for the sleaze, the embodiment of spinelessness.

Victoria Nulands—for the blood on their hands.

Extraction isn't war.

It doesn't leave visible casualties.

But on the grand scale of things, there is always a price—

Paid in blood, toil, tears and sweat.

Somewhere.

By someone.

JAMIE DIMON'S CONFESSION

've had bosses like Jamie Dimon.

The ones that came up through a system that rewards relentless discipline—summa cum laude, Harvard Business School, Wall Street's grind.

These men are hardened by early mornings and hard labor—convinced that work ethic alone is the key to everything. They believe in effort, in showing up, in "rolling up your sleeves."

Jamie Dimon's latest rant—leaked from an internal meeting—is a perfect artifact of executive delusion. Here's the best part:

"A lot of you were on the fucking Zoom and you were doing the following, okay? You know, looking at your mail, sending texts to each other about what an asshole the other person is, okay?"

He's furious. He thinks workers should be engaged, focused, hanging on his every word. That's how work should be, right? Except...

"If I was running a department for one hundred people, I guarantee you if I wanted to, I could run it with ninety and be more efficient. I guarantee you. I could do it in my sleep."

Wait. So he knows the workforce is bloated. He knows it's inefficient. He knows he could run a department with 10% fewer people.

So why hasn't he?

Because corporate inefficiency isn't an accident. It's a feature.

And he doesn't actually want to fix it—he wants to rant about it. To signal that he's still in control, that he's the hard-nosed boss who "gets things done," that everyone else is the problem.

But you can hear it in the leaked audio—he feels things slipping. He wants to stay relevant. There's so much insecurity in his voice that, for a moment, I actually felt sorry for the billionaire.

God, they grow old too. And they become boys again—petulant, performative, still trying to prove something.

"Your people are going to meetings they don't need to go to. I can't stand it anymore... We didn't build this great company by doing that, by doing the same semi-disease shit that everybody else does."

"Semi-disease shit." Like Crohn's? JPMorgan Crohn.

Dimon's frustration isn't an insight—it's a confession.

His "lazy employees," endless Zoom calls, and the "semi-disease shit"?

That's not some external force corrupting JPMorgan.

That is JPMorgan.

That's the Proximity Economy.

AMERICA, INC.:
THE BUSINESS OF PROXIMITY

was seventeen when I first ate at McDonald's. It had just opened
in Novi Sad, Serbia—and it had one thing no other place did: air
conditioning. On hot days, I'd step inside after school to cool off.
Arches. I live in St. Louis. We have the Arch. It's beautiful. I like
the look of the golden arches too.

But when I see them now, I don't see arches—I see a little gold
house, planted on land.

McDonald's makes most of its profit not from food, but from
real estate. It owns the land, the buildings, and everything inside—
kiosks, bots, code.

Then leases it all to franchisees. I think of them as small business
owners—mom and pop—people who once had a dream: to open
something of their own. To feed people. To belong.

But Americans trust arches. They don't trust mom and pop.

Eventually, mom and pop realized they couldn't compete with
companies like McDonald's.

So they opened a McDonald's instead.

They pay McDonald's to use the land, the building, the logo, the
self-ordering kiosks.

They run the day-to-day: employees, sick days, shift coverage. All the friction.

If it touches a human, it's the mom and pop's problem.

But if it's land, buildings, kiosks, bots, or algorithms—McDonald's keeps it.

The more things get automated, the more control shifts back to McDonald's.

We stopped at McDonald's on our drive from St. Louis to Chicago the other day. There aren't many options besides fast food on I-55 North.

Instead of "What can I get you, ma'am?" I got: "We're cash only."

Why? Because cash is friction. Card is automation. But not just that.

An order taker is a human—and she's friction too. The kiosk is automation.

Her job becomes making herself obsolete—nudging us toward the machine.

There's one less worker on the floor because the kiosk handles the orders.

That's not extra profit for the mom and pop—it mostly flows to McDonald's.

One day, maybe not so far from now, when the last job is automated, the last order taken, the last burger flipped by a human hand—

McDonald's will own the entire "switch". No mom and pop. No friction.

Just a closed loop: asset to algorithm to revenue, over and over.

McDonald's doesn't want to run McDonald's.

They want to own the machine that runs McDonald's.

They want to be more like Mastercard.

Mastercard is already further along in this process. Its switch is more mature—contained, consolidated, with fewer intermediaries. It's a cleaner extraction machine.

But I still ask the same question about McDonald's that I ask about Mastercard:

Should access to the switch—literal, like at Mastercard, or symbolic, like McDonald's rent-seeking built on land, brand, and self-ordering kiosks—be permanent? Inherited? Rent-generating forever, until the end of time?

The people working the grills at McDonald's are no different from the Switch maintenance workers at Mastercard. They do real jobs. They cook our food. They're underpaid.

The people at McDonald's Headquarters? They belong to the same class as the ones at Mastercard.

They're land, brand, and algorithmic aristocrats.

They skim from the top. They never sweat.

I've never worked at McDonald's Headquarters. I didn't need to. It's the same business model.

If there's a corporate campus with fountains and neatly mown lawns, odds are it's full of Nothing People.

We scroll. We eat lunch outside, facing the fountains. The rush of water is soothing.

Sometimes we take our laptops out and call it "working in nature."

Sometimes we get restless—so companies offer gardening.

At Mastercard, we had plots where we could grow tomatoes and take them home to our families.

We grow vegetables and feel a little less like Nothing People.

And that's if we even go to campus—because many of us work from home.

At Mastercard, surplus extraction created workers performing mostly fake jobs. At McDonald's, real jobs are being replaced by kiosks—so the bullshit jobs at headquarters keep multiplying.

But now AI threatens the programmers. And the office workers. Even the ones with fake jobs.

If AI agents start replacing people performing illusions, will they eventually automate the illusion itself?

It's a big question—but not the one I'm trying to answer here.

The managerial class can't grow forever by manufacturing bullshit. What happens if the illusion finally collapses?

If the gatekeepers—the ones at the top—can no longer hide behind a fake-job workforce?

Maybe they want to shed that workforce too—just like McDonald's sheds order takers.

People are friction.

The next frontier, then, is energy.

AI still runs on electric power—and that power isn't cheap.

We may no longer have workers, but the networks will still demand energy: for maintenance, for scale, for all the so-called innovation.

That's what they'll point to. That's how they'll justify what's left of their control.

Yes, labor costs are down. But now energy costs are up. So we need to continue charging you fees.

One curtain may fall. But another—the one that's easier to manage—will rise.

With all those networks spreading globally, it hit me—this whole country is just one big damn switch.

Should it really be surprising that Trump is proposing a "gold card" for those who want to gain access? A work permit with a $5 million price tag, paid directly to the U.S. government.

The instinct is revealing: why not charge for access? For proximity?

It's also a sign: the low-hanging fruit of innovation is gone. The systems are built. Platforms locked in. Markets saturated. The odds of talented immigrants bringing something truly new? Slim.

We're not after your work or ideas anymore.

We're selling access—

To networks, institutions, and whatever scraps of leverage remain.

Because in America's mature economy, most of the value is already owned, branded, or automated.

What's left to sell... is proximity.

Once, a man asked my husband where he was from. My husband answered, and the man—probably just looking for confirmation that America means something to us—asked, "So you feel lucky to be here?"

My husband said: "Of course, I feel lucky. Do you feel lucky to be here? I'm here by choice. By someone's permission. I put up effort to come here. I left people I love behind. I had to assimilate.

You should feel even more lucky," he said. "You were just born here. Isn't that luck?"

The guy just stood there, confused. I think he got his confirmation—just not in the way he expected.

But that exchange makes even more sense to me now. Americans are lucky to be born near the networks. Inside the switch. Inside America Inc.

I've been thinking about the people considering paying $5 million for a pathway into America.

Maybe they just want insurance—a safer base for their business.

If it's protection or privacy they're after, Montenegro offers the same deal for a fraction of the price. A few hundred thousand buys you citizenship, a dock for your yacht, and front-row views of the bluest waters on the Adriatic.

If it's prestige they're chasing—or access to elite networks for their kids—sure, they might get that here.

But they'll also get a fragmented society. A signaling economy. A place where even the top schools prepare them for roles that feel like performance art.

I don't know how that makes sense.

Maybe I'm the one missing something.

I always thought that once you crossed a certain income threshold, the game changed. It wasn't about access anymore—it was about staying grounded. Staying somewhere real. A place with extended family. Friends from childhood. Where someone still makes you soup when you're sick. Where there are still mom-and-pop restaurants. Where there's still ownership, belonging, and the quiet beauty of small business—the aesthetics, the spirit of it. Like in the old America—before the networks, before fast food chains turned into global conglomerates.

Some might say, "Yeah, but we get cheap prices."

But if there were no McDonald's, prices could still be cheap—not because of scale, but because of competition. More small restaurants. More variety. Lower prices.

And we'd have our favorites to cherish. To talk about. To visit. To enjoy.

We'd be greeted with, "Hi. What are you having today?" instead of, "This register is cash only."

That way the money would stay in the community.

It wouldn't float upward to the Nothing People and their campuses.

Novi Sad's main square is called Trg Slobode—Freedom Square.

It has a cathedral and is framed by Austro-Hungarian facades.

Pigeons rest on the statue of a man who fought for the freedom of Serbs in the Austro-Hungarian Empire. That Freedom Square once held an eyesore called McDonald's—where I stopped to cool off on my way home from school.

Thankfully, it's gone now.

Somehow, the square freed itself.

I want to believe someone started paying attention.

Because that's what it takes—attention. Otherwise, the system spreads. Quietly. Like mold.

First, a square. Then a town. Then a country lulled into believing there's no alternative.

We get ease, we get automation—but it dulls something. The best parts of us fall asleep. The worst parts start to speak.

In the Proximity Economy, that worst part sounds like a Nothing Person saying, "Our cash coffers are full."

In the real economy, it's the cashier at McDonald's saying, "It's cash only."

I don't think Americans want it to be this way.

But it simply is.

When I came to America, the U.S. government—or really, the taxpayers—funded my education through a Pell Grant, a federal scholarship for low-income students.

It was American taxpayers who covered my classes at UTA.

I took out some loans, but most of it was paid.

I don't know how we got from that—that image of Americans investing in a smart refugee like me to this.

I was supposed to build something real.

Maybe create jobs.

Or at least contribute to society by doing a real job.

But here I am, absorbed into the Proximity Economy—participating in the extraction, writing about golden arches, gold cards, and how America became one big switch.

I've just added to the decay.

It's such an uninspiring immigrant story.

I hate it.

SCENE: KLUB
KNJIŽEVNIKA, BELGRADE

The place of Yugoslavia's greatest writers still holds onto its quiet dignity. A low murmur of conversation, the soft clink of porcelain cups, the occasional scent of fresh flowers on the tables.

A chessboard sits between them, pieces untouched. Two cappuccinos, nearly empty.

Stabilist glances at the elegantly dressed patrons, taking in the scene.

Dynamist leans back, exhaling, watching the candlelight flicker against the framed portraits of long-dead poets—men who once sat in this very space, or out under the trees on a day as beautiful as this one.

They are waiting for the best krempita[16] in the world.

> **Dynamist:** You're calling it "stabilism" now? What happened to statism?

> **Stabilist:** Statism sounds like central control. Stabilism is about stopping motion for motion's sake. It's not about centralizing power—it's about stopping innovation

---

16. Krempita: A Balkan custard dessert with layers of cream and puff pastry. Not just a dessert—a cultural inheritance.

signaling and pointless churn. Two-thirds of the economy
runs on inherited digital machinery. Bloated hierarchies
exist just to sustain themselves. We don't need more noise.
We need to stabilize, cut the dead weight, and refocus on
what creates value.

Dynamist: You act like stagnation is some grand crisis, but
isn't that just alarmism? Look at AI, biotech, and green
energy. Entire industries are transforming before our eyes.

Stabilist: A third of the economy, sure. The other two-
thirds? Stagnating. And remember, it wasn't some stabilist economist who pointed this out—it was your favorite
dynamist, Tyler Cowen. For every breakthrough in biotech,
there are hundreds of transactions AUTHED, CLEARED,
and SETTLED by a Switch built back when Nixon was
president.

Dynamist: (smiling) Is there such a thing as a stabilist
economist?

Stabilist: Maybe not officially. But Piketty, perhaps. Or
Varoufakis—he'd torch the proximity economy without
blinking.

Dynamist: (nodding) Fair point. But inefficiencies are part
of capitalism's genius. They attract disruptors—people
who see an opening, exploit it, and force change. That's
creative destruction.

Stabilist: (smiling faintly) You'd have a point if disrupt-
ers were allowed to disrupt. In just the last five years,

Mastercard has made thirty-two acquisitions, Visa eighteen. Visa even tried to acquire Plaid, its biggest emerging competitor, in 2020—until the DOJ stepped in. And what happens to the products these companies create? Many get shelved, not scaled.

Dynamist: (leaning forward) You act like proximity giants don't innovate. Look at Mastercard's blockchain projects, or Visa's advancements in fraud detection. That's real innovation.

Stabilist: (raising an eyebrow) It's mostly innovation signaling. (Hands over a book.) Read this book—*Fatamorgana*. The so-called advancements? Mostly just minor tweaks to existing systems. Mastercard alone has buried more innovations through acquisitions than it's ever launched.

Dynamist: (laughing) You sound like you want to regulate the entire economy. Make everything a public utility, strip away competition. How's that worked for the Post Office?

Stabilist: (sharply) Not the entire economy, the focus is on two-thirds—the part that's stagnating. And what do we have now? Legacy systems that already freeze the economy in place! Stabilism doesn't mean stifling risk—it means rebalancing power so that progress isn't hoarded by those closest to the machinery. More companies in this stagnating financial world need to be turned to Public utilities so they don't suppress value; they ensure it benefits everyone. And since you mentioned the Post Office, read your favorite dynamist economist Tyler Cowen's article titled "Privatize the USPS? Not in the era of Crony Capitalism". The title says it all.

Dynamist: (pausing, stirring their coffee) Okay, but stagnation isn't just inefficiency. It's natural. We've picked the low-hanging fruit. Of course, innovation slows as the easy problems are solved.

Stabilist: (leaning forward, voice measured) Agreed, some ceilings are natural. But inefficiency amplifies stagnation. When resources flow into extracting value from legacy systems instead of pursuing new frontiers, we're not just slowed by the ceiling—we're weighed down by the inertia of inefficiency.

Dynamist: (narrowing eyes) But your view reduces humans to cogs in a machine. Where's the agency, the creativity? People break systems all the time.

Stabilist: (smiling) True, but incentives shape agency. The Proximity Economy rewards signaling over substance. It doesn't suppress creativity outright—it redirects it into activities that sustain the status quo. Human agency is alive, but if wealth and power flow not from innovation, but from proximity to inherited systems, gatekeeping, and the illusion of progress, then Houston, we have a problem.

Dynamist: (sitting back, arms crossed) So what's your solution? Nationalize the Switch?

Stabilist: (calmly, with a faint smile) My solution is simple: divide and conquer. Let the innovative third of the economy thrive under traditional market dynamics. But for the stagnant two-thirds? Apply stabilism where the economy is stuck—where it's just extraction, not creation. Reclassify certain industries as public utilities. Break up dominant players—like AT&T in the '80s. It didn't destroy the industry; it revitalized it. Regulate entrenched rent-seekers—Big Tech, Big Finance—where consolidation has replaced competition. And yes, fire a whole bunch of people—because half these jobs exist to perpetuate inefficiencies, not to create value. It's not about stifling markets; it's about untangling the Proximity Economy from the parts that still function.

Dynamist: Fire a whole bunch of people?

Stabilist: Yes. One email—subject line: "Fork in the Road."

It sucks.

But pretending is worse.

Dynamist: That sounds… brutal.

Stabilist: What's brutal is paying salaries just to sustain the illusion of work. Besides, they'll be fine—most of them are already on LinkedIn posting thought leadership about resilience.

Dynamist: You talk about breaking up stagnation like it's easy. But intervention doesn't always fix things—it can make them worse. Look at 2008. The government stepped in, bailed out the banks, and what did we get? More consolidation, not less.

Stabilist: That's because we bailed them out instead of restructuring them.

Dynamist: You talk about utilities, but look at Texas's energy market as proof that deregulation works.

Stabilist: Texas has a lot of sun. People can go off-grid. You don't just "go off-grid" from Visa and Mastercard. (And they're not the only ones.) You need access to the system to function in daily life.

Dynamist: But what stops that from turning into a slippery slope? Who's to say what's stagnation and what's just the natural slowdown of progress?

Stabilist: Sometimes, the world genuinely changes. It's not a slippery slope; it's recognizing when the old rules don't work anymore.

Dynamist: (leaning back, skeptical) So you think a touch of stabilism will fix it?

Stabilist: (with conviction) Not fix. Adjust. Adapt. Call it an evolution of capitalism, if that makes it easier to accept. Keep the dynamism where it works, intervene where it's calcified—where it's crony capitalism. It's not about control. It's about unsticking a system that's frozen in place.

Dynamist: (smirking slightly) Sounds like you're building a museum, not an economy.

Stabilist: (smirking back) If these companies are still around in fifty years, maybe we should open them up as museums. Why not?

A spoon dips into the krempita. The best in the world. Soft, layered, perfectly balanced.

Dynamist (smirks, gesturing to the krempita). Some things hit the ceiling—and don't need to be disrupted.

Stabilist (smirks, taking a bite). We finally agreed.

THE EMPIRE
HAS NO FACTORY

LIVING THROUGH THE DEI ERA

I n 2020, after the killing of George Floyd, corporate America embraced DEI—diversity, equity, inclusion—as its moral north star. Wokeness, once a call for awareness, hardened into branding. The protests on the streets felt real—raw, chaotic, human. But inside the corporate walls, it looked hollow from the start.

Middle managers had purpose again—finally, a people problem. They could play leaders.

HR loved it. DEI gave them edge.

Higher-ups scrambled, unsure how to respond. They watched what other executives were doing, called PR firms, tried to calculate what dollar amount might appease the moment.

My coworkers were just waiting—refreshing inboxes, dissecting every word of the CEO's statement.

Ajay Banga finally issued one.

He said he 'saw' us. Heard us. Felt discrimination himself.

But there was no money. Just words.

And people were fuming.

Later, Mastercard launched the *In Solidarity* initiative—pledging millions to Black-owned small businesses, financial inclusion efforts, community partnerships.

But the money was spaced out over years. You never give a lump sum.

Because cultural winds change.

They hired Chief Diversity Officers, and filled our calendars with weekly progress meetings. My boss scheduled a separate meeting titled "Support Our Teammates." I attended the first one and then sent him an email outlining why I wouldn't attend the next one. I saved that email. Looking back, I suspect I was thinking—if this keeps snowballing and I end up in HR one day, I'd like to have some receipts.

Five years later, I cringe—not at the words, but at the fact that I felt the need to write them. But it stands as an artifact of its time:

I said I would write my thoughts about that meeting, so here it is.

I realize that everyone is so sensitive nowadays, so I hesitate to say anything. Yet again, that Zoom Team Meeting we've had on Thursday left me wondering: "Um, what just happened?" You gave us a preview in the invite; the meeting was optional; you mentioned we are not therapists, that a meeting was a gathering of friends and teammates to talk, to express our feelings, etc. For that reason, I feel I should have known what was coming, but again, I couldn't fully predict that the conversation would go that way.

Here are a few things that took me by surprise:

> *1. I never thought I would be listening to my coworkers cry in a meeting while describing their personal experiences with racial bias. I know many people are hurting now, and I realize that corporate America is under pressure*

to respond. Still, I wonder if this is a new normal. We've had tragic events in the past, but this is the first time I've had a meeting scheduled at the workplace to discuss events and people's personal experience in such raw form.

2. *I never thought I would listen to a coworker so openly criticize top leadership for failing to respond more compellingly and concretely.*

3. *I never thought I would hear you apologizing for being "just a 46-year-old white male from Midwest" who will be careful not to "whitesplain" but instead "listen and learn." Should we really limit our insights and contributions to matters that align with our race, age, or gender? I reject the assumption that your whiteness prohibits sensitivity and sound judgment, or that others' race guarantees them. Or that people of color on our team must somehow feel more pain watching the senseless death of George Floyd than white people. It reduces people to their identity and ignores their complexity.*

4. *You recommended "White Fragility." I read parts of it, but found the concept troubling.*

A part of me worries about seeing this mindset take root in the workplace. I hope this theory never gains traction at Mastercard.

I know you've had the best intentions in mind; you wanted us all to support our coworkers who might be hurting—we show up, listen, and they hopefully feel better. I hope it helped them, although I think it probably made no difference. I will opt out of future meetings of this kind. I hope that's OK.

That was my email then—written in the middle of a storm I didn't fully understand.

Later, I sent more emails. One to the Chief People Officer, after the boss of my boss encouraged us to "go out on the streets." He replied with something bland—polite, vaguely patronizing, forgettable.

Funny how a passing vibe can expose just how equally flawed we all are.

During and after the Bosnian war, which was ethnic in nature, people didn't just sort each other by identity—they displaced, excluded, and killed.

I was a child from a mixed marriage—which, at the time, was more inconvenient than exotic.

In Serbia, my father's name made me the other. In Bosnia, it was my mother's name—or my Serbian license plates.

In high school, I briefly lived in a boarding dorm and had to change rooms after my roommate found out my dad was a Bosniak.

"I escaped from them," she said, "and now I have to live with one."

I wasn't devastated. Just annoyed that I had to pack up and move.

Now that I think about it, why was I the one who had to leave? Why didn't she?

It never even crossed my mind until now.

Those dorm attendants should have known better.

The Balkans had changed. People don't ask anymore. Everyone celebrates their own holidays, lives mostly within their ethnic lines—and that's just how it works now. Not ideal, not terrible. Just stable.

Of course, America isn't Bosnia in the '90s—but the logic underneath—the dividing, sorting, and shaming—felt uncomfortably familiar:

— "I am just a white man from the Midwest."

— Coworkers crying on Zoom, sharing what they'd lived through—and who they believed they were.

— School moms became social enforcers, wielding *White Fragility* like doctrine.

No, it wasn't the same. Bosnia was bloody—but we were at least authentic. America was just weird.

But it didn't stop at work—it followed me home.

A Facebook spat between two moms spiraled into a full-blown brawl. One accused a white teacher of favoring white kids. There was some kind of school investigation. I asked the secretary—she shrugged. I asked other moms—got fragments.

It was our teacher. He'd taught my daughter. I'd seen firsthand how he treated all students fairly. I knew these moms. They were caught in the moment, caught in the fever. But fairness didn't matter. The outrage machine was already rolling.

Then the white mom "allies" jumped in, outdoing each other in accusations and moral posturing. They called me a racist. Told me to "check my privilege."

I wasn't quiet, of course. I called all of them—white allies and Black accusers alike—ignorant, self-righteous, and embarrassingly American.

Yes, it was harsh. But I was pissed.

They demanded I take the school's Anti-Bias, Anti-Racist (ABAR) training. That I read *White Fragility*. That I "open my eyes."

One of the Black moms brought up slavery. She didn't know my background. I didn't know hers. But I'd bet my kids are fewer generations removed from forced labor than hers.

When World War II broke out, German forces entered Bosnian villages and took civilians to work on farms while German men went off to fight. Whether they were technically classified as POWs or not, they were treated as human capital for a war machine. These villagers weren't paid—they were simply taken. Forced laborers. Slaves.

My husband's grandfather Nedjo—an ethnic Serb—was one of them. He left behind a wife and five children. He returned after the war. He was lucky. The other grandfather with the same name, also a Serb and a miner, wasn't. He was killed by the Ustaše—his fellow miners. It took over twenty years to bring those responsible to justice. A trial was held, and they began serving prison sentences in the 1970s.

My mother's uncle, Dušan, was nineteen, serving as a sailor in the navy of the Kingdom of Yugoslavia, stationed in Montenegro. When Italy occupied the region, he was captured and deported to Italy, where he was forced to work in vineyards—slave labor, again.

My other great uncle, Ilo, either died or was taken during the Kozara offensive, when German and Ustaše forces swept through the region. Many civilians were killed; others were deported to concentration camps.

My grandparents spent their youth in the forests, hiding from German forces, trying not to be killed.

The Balkan peoples are mostly South Slavs. My family—we are all Slavs. And for centuries, Slavs have been treated as disposable labor. Even the word *"slave"* comes from *"Slav."* We were the original slaves. Long before the transatlantic trade, Slavs were captured and sold across Europe—by Turks, Arabs, and others. It was practiced on my people long before it was practiced on hers.

But tell Americans long enough that they're an exceptional nation, and they start claiming it for everything.

No, it's not a contest. It shouldn't be.

But that Black mom was the one making assumptions—not me.

Other moms I knew well sat on the sidelines, watching as the Facebook group filled with public condemnations. Some cowered in silence. Others quietly cosigned the mob with *likes*. It was disappointing—how quickly people I'd known for years joined in, or stayed silent.

Watching all of that play out here, in polite America, was surreal.

Kids stopped getting birthday invitations. And they noticed.

You didn't have to be a professor teaching a controversial syllabus to be canceled.

In the end, my husband and I tapped our savings, left our house in a diverse neighborhood, and moved to a condo in a wealthier area called Clayton. New district. New school.

Social media fights with moms don't come cheap.

And now, in 2025, the tide has turned.

Wokeness has collapsed.

Tech bros run the block now.

"Apollo took over from Cybele."

Corporate DEI is being dismantled.

Even liberal publications are questioning what they once amplified.

The air is shifting.

The Columbus statue still hasn't returned to Tower Grove Park, where it stood for more than a century.

I used to take my kids there.

When they took it down that summer in 2020, my daughter noticed.

"Mom, where's the statue?"

"It's gone, honey. But it'll be back in ten years."

Five to go.

And yet—my view has softened.

Why not DEI?

If the jobs are performative, if working in these corporations is mostly innovation signaling—why not let it lean toward those historically left out? We might as well signal for something.

It won't fix the machinery, but it might ease the guilt—the kind only salaried people get to feel.

DEI was never a threat to the real machinery.

It was a diversion—useful when the winds demanded it, quietly abandoned when meritocracy became cool again.

But the business of business never changed.

Still rent-seeking. Still extracting. Still calling it business.

And that's always been the most interesting thing to me about these corporations: not how people show up, not what their identity needs are—but the business model. The bottom line.

THE ILLUSION OF CHOICE

BigTech didn't replace OldTech. It feeds off it.

OldTech processes money. BigTech processes attention.

One extracts silently. The other pulls you in.

OldTech doesn't move fast—but it doesn't need to. It keeps running—outlasting trends, outliving its builders, resisting every attempt to change it.

The old power still sits in OldTech: the humming servers of Visa, Mastercard, Goldman Sachs, and JPMorgan.

They dictate who profits, who gets funded, who gets locked out.

BigTech is the new Leviathan.

It decides what we see, what we buy, what we value—one scroll at a time.

It doesn't just process money. It controls attention, identity, behavior.

Unlike OldTech, which extracts in the background, BigTech seduces.

Its power is less rigid, more fluid.

The core remains untouched—but now it's networked, mined, manipulated.

OldTech behaves like an oligopoly—banks and clearinghouses feeding into the same rails, credit networks passing through the same two giants.

BigTech behaves like a collection of monopolies.

Google owns search.

Meta owns social.

Amazon owns cloud.

Apple owns devices.

They don't just control their spaces—they shape how we move through them.

OldTech: *"I need my bank, my credit card, my paycheck."*

BigTech: *"I want my phone, my apps, my notifications."*

You are all locked in. I like that term. It comes from aviation—that moment when a pilot locks onto a target. The target is secured, unable to escape.

In big financial and banking corporations, we used *lock-in* to describe what happens to customers. For inherited digital machinery, we used *sticky*. The switch is sticky. The network is sticky. Meaning you—the customer—can't leave so easily. There's dependency.

This is how we talk about you, the customer. *Retention. Friction. Barriers to exit.* We engineer dependency so you can't escape.

The best business model isn't the one that attracts customers; it's the one that traps them. Like a spider traps a fly in its web.

Not through addiction—that's BigTech's domain. BigTech is about wants. You want to be on Facebook, Instagram, Amazon. You want engagement. You want convenience.

OldTech is different. OldTech doesn't hook you through dopamine. It traps you through necessity. You need to buy. You need to pay. You need to receive your paycheck. So you need a bank account.

Which means you need Bank of America. Chase. Visa and Master-card. There is no opt-out.

And to be clear, this isn't a call to be Luddites. The technology itself isn't the enemy—it's the way it's used as a proxy for extraction by algorithmic aristocrats.

You are the target. And they've locked you in.

Platinum or Gold? Pick your card. They profit either way.

You can't say "I'm done with TransUnion, I'm taking my data to Equifax." That's not how it works.

PayPal offers money transfer in seconds—for five dollars. Or wait three days—for free.

If you pick free, they hold the funds, profit off the float.

We all know it: Time is money. Money is time. Nothing's free.

Credit card holders think they're gaming the system—earning air miles, cash back.

No. You're just a minor participant in a rent-extraction model.

And those without cards—who pay with cash, checks, or food stamps?

Usually the poorest among us.

They receive no salary from the system. They receive no stock valuations like shareholders.

No points. No perks. But they still pay.

Banks fund rewards by charging merchants high fees.

Merchants pass those fees to consumers—baked into higher prices for everyone.

So the poorest among us pay the most. They get nothing in return.

It's all too complex for the average person to follow.

It's not transparent—so most people never see it.
And financial companies profit from that complexity.
Because complexity isn't always organic.
Often, it's engineered—to shield the machine.

THE LEVIATHANS
OF STAGNATION

We had generous salaries—$250K to $300K a year.
In Missouri, after tax, that's the price of a decent house.
If your spouse worked too, you could afford one every year.

But labor costs for Mastercard were a rounding error.

Like the fourth decimal of pi—technically there, but nobody cares.

They generated tens of billions in profit—without factories, without warehouses, without the drag of real operational costs.

So where did the profits go?

Just here and there.

Dividends. Stock buybacks.

Acquisitions—a giant vacuum sucking up potential threats before they could grow.

Executive compensation, naturally.

And filling more coffers.

Louis Vuitton bags stuffed with cash.

A sign over the vault: "No Peasants Allowed."

Vanity plates on Ferraris out front: PKTCHNG.

(Kidding. Sort of.)

Mastercard's Priceless Experiences just launched in the Philippines.

I traveled there twice—business class, of course. Luxury hotel. Personal driver. Here I'm not kidding.

They posted a video from the opening. They had reserved the museum as the venue:

"We made it a multisensory affair—spice-infused, with a sense of Mastercard's iconic fragrances: passionate optimism, a string quartet playing songs from our sonic album, stunning visual displays, and of course, prominent branding."

Close-ups of the venue. Lavish dinner. Flower arrangements. Caviar. Cocktails.

Locals holding umbrellas over the marketing lady—because it's raining.

Priceless Experiences is Mastercard's luxury branding campaign that promotes curated events designed to make spending feel like culture, and elite consumption feel like connection.

There are some things money can't buy...
Indeed.

Visa and Mastercard's profit margins are staggering—50%.

Half of every dollar they make is pure profit.

It's not magic. It's math.

For every $100 I earned for doing nothing, Mastercard needed to skim one cent from 10,000 people.

A tiny amount, barely noticeable—but $100 is tiny too.

Now scale it up: our collective salaries—an entire company, an industry, two-thirds of the economy. The entire global economy.

Musa al-Gharabi calls it "symbolic capitalism"[17].

People like me—he calls us symbolic capitalists. He admits he is one too.

He shows with data how finance, insurance, and real estate—the largest sector—produce nothing tangible.

They extract rents or bet on what might become valuable downstream.

"A system where elites derive wealth and power not through production, but by managing narratives, affiliations, and appearances."

Al-Gharbi is an academic, so he describes it as "managing narratives, affiliations, and appearances."

I'm a corporate insider.

I call it innovation signaling.

Same thing.

A trillion-dollar industry built on fluff.

What is fluff?

It boils down to trust—outsourced.

We fear each other. We fear risk.

So we hand it over to companies.

And they monetize it.

---

17. *We Have Never Been Woke* (2024) by Musa al-Gharbi.

THE EMPIRE EXTRACTS BACK

Every year, I return to Europe for a few months. I work remotely when I'm there. In tech, we've mastered the art of appearing productive from across the globe.

I spend my time in the Balkans—Serbia, Montenegro, Croatia— where most of my extended family lives, and where the land still feels familiar, hospitable—like it remembers me. Two years ago, we spent a few months on Hvar Island in Croatia. The bakery closed at eleven, the museum at one, the cathedral at two, the pharmacy at four. Everything shut down on Sunday. There's a rhythm, a pace to life—and it makes sense. Sundays are for rest, family, church— not for shopping at the mall. Thankfully, there are no malls anyway.

When Americans want to feel good about their economy, they point to Europe—a continent of short workdays, siestas, aging populations, and a lack of innovation. Their brightest youth don't stay; they're lured away by American corporations, universities, and the promise of entrepreneurial spirit. The narrative is flattering. And maybe true.

Trump talks about tariffs, about unfair trade. Macron pushed back—Trump wasn't counting services: financial, search, streaming, consulting. I've seen the reports at Mastercard—the outflows. Macron has a point. A huge chunk of wealth Europe generates is funneled outward through services.

Interchange and network fees, cross-border charges, data monetization, licensing costs, cloud infrastructure payments, consulting fees, profit repatriation—it all adds up.

Visa and Mastercard, Google, Meta, Amazon, Apple, McKinsey, Accenture, JPMorgan, Goldman Sachs, FedEx, Netflix—you see them everywhere. So-called global companies—until you follow the money. Then it's clear: they're still very much American.

In 2022, we were at Jahorina, a ski resort in Bosnia. The sheer scale of Mastercard's branding was overwhelming. Massive banners surrounded the ski center. The ticket counters might as well have been wrapped in their logo. It was intrusive, almost offensive—something foreign invading a space that should have felt local and untouched. The aesthetics were terrible. Their bold red and yellow logos might work in sleek urban settings, but against green pines and fresh snow, they clashed like a loud voice in a library.

My husband reminded me that it was my Mastercard salary that brought us here to ski.

"Shouldn't you snap a photo in front of these Mastercard banners," he said, "and post it on LinkedIn with something like, 'Thank you, #Mastercard, for this priceless experience'?"

He can be funny.

Why is Europe so willing to surrender the flow of commerce, credit, and capital—the very rails on which its entire economy runs—to U.S. corporations? Do they not realize that every Visa and Mastercard transaction swiped in Europe literally travels across the ocean for slicing and trimming before it's sent back to Europe? Americans take a slice. European banks take their cut, too.

Imagine a siphon hooked up to the European economy. Water gets sucked in, travels across the ocean, rounds through the U.S., where Visa and Mastercard take their cut—just a small leak. Then, on its way back to Europe, a few more holes appear—European banks extracting their share. By the time the water is pumped back, it's no longer a steady flow. It sputters, like a garden hose with air pockets. Europe created a company that could have fixed the leak. Mastercard acquired it—and kept the leak open.

In 2017, while I was at Mastercard, the company acquired Vocalink, a UK firm that built the Faster Payments infrastructure. Internally, the deal was celebrated as a strategic move to diversify our portfolio.

As part of the post-acquisition integration team, I flew to London to learn about Vocalink's IPS switch. A room full of architects from both sides—parent company Mastercard and the acquired Vocalink—gathered around whiteboards, mapping the switch's anatomy that powered the UK economy.

After the meeting, back in my hotel, questions surfaced: Why acquire something that competes with our core card services? We already had similar capabilities. It wasn't long before leadership started discussing how scaling Vocalink might cannibalize our core card services in the consumer-to-merchant space.

The acquisition, it became clear, wasn't about synergy—it was about neutralizing a competitor that could jeopardize Mastercard's dominance in the European card market.

Vocalink was a European invention, a model of financial sovereignty. It had the potential to help EU countries replicate the UK's Faster Payments system, keeping control over their financial infrastructure and reducing reliance on foreign players like Mastercard and Visa.

What happened to this switch, which by the way was more modern, modular, and built on the latest ISO 20022[18] payment standard? Despite its technical sophistication, the switch was quietly absorbed.

Its real-world potential—for helping countries build sovereign payment rails—was diluted.

Vocalink's website doesn't even mention that early ambition.

The focus has shifted. "Card Transaction Services" and managed offerings now dominate.

The independence is gone. The potential—killed.

Years later, Mastercard ran the same play with Scandinavian Nets' account-to-account payment business. The European Commission scrutinized the deal, but it still let the deal close.

Mastercard's leadership, meanwhile, has been strikingly candid about their intentions. In an annual CEO letter, their strategy was described as "extending into adjacent spaces and networks to leave no white space uncontested." It's a clear acknowledgment of their drive not just to grow, but to ensure no competitor can gain a foothold.

What they do is systematic consolidation. Like Pac-Man on an endless loop, gobbling up everything in their path—startups, competitors, ideas. Not to scale them. To swallow them.

Internally at Mastercard, I often heard a phrase that encapsulated this vision: "We are the network of networks."

It wasn't just about payments anymore. It was about everything—identity, data flows, consumers, small business, large business.

Total integration. Total control.

Big countries like China and Russia want nothing to do with foreign payment systems. To them, Visa and Mastercard are American infrastructure. Dependence isn't just risky—it's unthinkable. Payment

---

18. ISO 20022 enables richer, more structured financial data than older card messaging formats like ISO 8583.

rails are as essential as highways or power grids. This isn't just about protecting finances; it's about safeguarding sovereignty.

Imagine if Russia didn't have MIR, its own payment network, when the war in Ukraine began. When Visa and Mastercard cut off services, MIR kept the domestic economy functioning. Without it, the consequences would've been far worse.

Europe, meanwhile, has taken the opposite approach. As Macron lamented in a recent speech, "No other region in the world, other than Europe, would have accepted, to the extent that we do, to be dependent on others for vital products and essential components."

Why is Europe allowing this? Who benefits? Why is there no resistance?

Just recently, Mastercard's CEO co-hosted a fancy dinner in Germany, standing before a room of Eurocrats with a microphone in hand. Later, he shared a polished LinkedIn post about the evening:

"Transatlantic partnership is key to building geopolitical relationships, strong global trade, and societal resilience—all of which help create a digital economy that works for everyone, everywhere."

But how is it a partnership when the transatlantic connection only flows one way—from Europe to the U.S.? It's not collaboration; it's U.S.-based corporate power wrapped in the warm, friendly guise of unity.

There's a reason the CEO of the "network of networks" no longer sounds like a business leader. He runs a corporation with too much power. His job isn't business—it's politics. Those words should be coming from a Secretary of State, not the head of a payment company.

As long as Visa and Mastercard are flush with foreign revenue, they remain untouchable to regulators.

U.S. regulator knocks on the door: "Why are you extracting all these fees?"

Visa and Mastercard: "But we're a global company, don't you know? We bring in outflows from Europe."

U.S. regulator: "Oh, I see. Carry on."

If Europe can't process payments without U.S. intermediaries, how sovereign is it, really?

It built better railroads than America. Financial ones should've been easier.

And yet—it's still plugged into the American switch.

The EU has started fining Big Tech, which is something:

Apple: €500 million. Meta: €200 million.

It should fine Old Tech too—Visa, Mastercard.

But Trump didn't applaud. He called it "overseas extortion."

As if Europe were the one extracting.

It sounded like something Tim Cook whispered to him—palms sweating over the fine, clutching his iPhone.

No. The real extraction isn't coming from Europe.

Just look at their GDP. Trillions are missing.

It's coming from Cupertino. From Menlo Park.

From the symbolic class right here at home.

Reclaiming financial sovereignty wouldn't just be a win for Europe.

It would be a warning shot—the first real fracture in the empire of American extractopolies.

Maybe even the beginning of something new.

OFFSHORING AND OTHER POWER PLAYS

OFFSHORE, REBRAND, REPEAT

When I left Mastercard for Wipro, an Indian IT giant, I took my noise-creating skills to a whole new level. I joined their sales team, tasked with overseeing the Mastercard account. They paid me more than Mastercard ever did. They grilled me on technical matters and seemed confident that my supposedly strong relationships would translate into new deals.

Sure, I knew a lot of people. Plenty didn't like me, and they had their reasons. What managers in Wipro didn't know—and what I didn't freely disclose—was that I was an employee who had cycled through PIPs. And now, I was supposed to bring in sales for them. Good luck with that.

Wipro had 1,350 employees embedded at Mastercard, tangled in the system. That number—1,350—was a carefully kept secret in pitches to Mastercard executives. You don't let the scale show. Too big, and execs might start asking questions—about efficiency, dependency, or who was really in control. Instead, we framed ourselves as indispensable partners, offering "cost savings through onshore-offshore balance" and "accelerators" to amplify Mastercard's operations. These so-called accelerators weren't innovative—they were carefully packaged noise: prebuilt dashboards with dummy data that looked like customer data, automation libraries, slide decks about "AI readiness."

Wipro wasn't just playing the game—it was milking it, extracting $150 million a year from Mastercard. And now, *somehow*, I was on their team.

Firms like TCS, Infosys, Cognizant, and HCLTech found their foothold by tapping into discretionary budgets—taking on low-priority work. But over time, they reshaped the work itself.

More offshore developers, more teams, more layers of process. They didn't just fill gaps. They manufactured them. More apps, more features, more repackaging—always cheaper, always "new." Quicker and cheaper than anyone else, they peeled off existing core services, wrapped them in new branding, and sold them back to the same companies as "innovation."

Offshoring surged after COVID, when work moved to homes and Zoom calls. Managers no longer needed to justify their roles by surrounding themselves with physical teams—visibility was gone. If no one could see who was in the building, why not hire offshore? So they shifted the game. They outsourced more labor. That became their cover: projects that were too cheap to cut, just complex enough to defend. Offshoring thrived. And the managers stayed.

And as reliance deepened, consulting firms found new ways to sustain and expand it. These firms don't just sustain dependency; they engineer it—thriving on FOMO, manufactured risks, opaque processes, and a deep understanding of human psychology. Their presence is most visible on LinkedIn, where they relentlessly tout "innovative" technologies. The pitch is always the same: "To fully reap the benefits of your investment, it's essential to replace the legacy core with a new technology stack," they proclaim. "Sticking to the old system will prevent you from realizing the full potential of cutting-edge technologies like AI."

Before AI, it was the cloud. Before that, virtualization. Before that, something else. The budgets grew, but the core—the real backbone—never changed.

It was never about hiring "the best." It was about cost and control.

But Mastercard changed too. A new managerial class had emerged—predominantly Indian. They rose through the ranks by hiring almost exclusively within their networks, creating a closed-loop system of homogeneity. It was no surprise they preferred to work with their own in a cheaper offshore model.

The new class brought traits like industriousness, collectivism, and respect for hierarchy—traits that can drive productivity in environments where real work is done. But in companies operating in Proximity Economy, those same traits became tools for reinforcing the status quo.

Lately, offshore companies have started benefiting from a new trend: "descaling."

That's what we called it internally—never in front of clients.

"The client is descaling. They need our help."

Here's what it means:

Banks A, B, C, and D all used vendor X for the same software.

Now they each want to build it in-house.

The reasoning?

ChatGPT makes code cheap.

They want more control.

They've got discretionary budget.

And their managers and IT teams are restless—they need something to do.

They can save on licensing fees.

So… why not?

They burn cash rebuilding what already exists.

Now, instead of one shared system from vendor X, there are four redundant versions—one at each bank.

No one questions the sunk cost.

Or the technical debt piling up beneath the surface.

Offshoring firms don't mind. They get a slice of the descaling pie.

Carefully scoped statements of work,

artfully pitched over expensive dinners—

low light, soft music.

Signed over *Bésame Mucho.*

THE INDIAN
WORKPLACE DYNAMIC

ike me, many Indian managers and technologists carried a quiet awareness of being outsiders who had gained entry into privileged territory. We had a lot in common: the immigrant experience, an engineering mindset, the quiet drive to prove ourselves.

But when I transitioned from Mastercard to Indian IT consulting firms like Wipro and Synechron (Indian by origin, leadership and operational DNA)—where Indians made up 90% of the workforce—the dynamic changed. I struggled personally and professionally. Whatever solidarity I once felt evaporated fast.

The bosses openly criticized subordinates in front of others. Americans might do that too, but they soften it, wrap it in *we*— "We need to make sure this happens next time."

But now it was suddenly direct, even confrontational.

In my first week, I joined a sales call where my boss got berated by his boss:

"Tell me, did you deliver it? What have you been doing for the last two days? Where are the numbers?"

I started wondering—was this just cutthroat sales culture? Or an Indian workplace dynamic?

After the call, I hesitated. Should I go to my boss's office and check if he's OK? The human side of me said yes. The survival instinct— maybe not. At work, self-preservation overrides empathy.

Most of the deals were renewals anyway. The business flow was steady. So why the manufactured stress?

In the past, the account had to grow 12% year over year. But once an IT consulting company reaches a certain level of presence— once it's fully embedded, functioning like a parasite on the host —the fantasy of double-digit growth should fade. The firm had latched on completely. There was nothing left to mine.

Actually Mastercard isn't the host. It's already a leech, attached to the arteries of commerce. The consulting firms are just lampreys on that leech—draining the same blood twice.

But many senior managers didn't grasp this basic math—that an account can't grow forever. Or maybe they refused to.

Very quickly, I realized I wasn't going to sell anything. There was no white space left to uncover—no new ground to take. My job wasn't about driving new business; it was about making sure I got credit for the renewals. I wasn't competing with other consulting firms. I was competing with my own sales team.

In sales, you can't work in isolation. I still had to collaborate. But being the only one who looked like me—only non-Indian—it never felt natural. I always felt like I had to prove I belonged.

To do that, I focused on two things. First, I spoke just enough technical jargon to justify my title. And second, I was pretty sure my lack of a wedding ring fed certain assumptions. So, I'd casually mention that I'd been married for twenty-six years—we just never got rings. Some cultures might find that detail unremarkable, but with Indian men, it always earned a nod of approval—an unspoken signal that aligned with their values. The quickest way to gain respect.

And no, it wasn't all in my head.

Yet, despite that small connection, I often found myself excluded in ways that were hard to ignore. Whenever a big boss came to our office, I felt invisible. The Indian men gathered in a conference room, whiteboarding and discussing sales strategies with him, while I—the only senior director of sales not invited—sat just outside in my cubicle. No calendar invite. No casual ask. They walked past me, chatting among themselves, heading off to lunch together, never thinking of including me. It was isolating, and though I couldn't be sure if it was intentional, it was a clear signal of where I stood.

Then there were moments that went beyond exclusion —outright breaches of trust. I'd been working on a renewal deal worth $16 million—or at least I thought I was. It seemed straightforward: just renewing the same Statement of Work, with a few minor additions. But the sales order never cleared under my name.

Puzzled, I reached out to the administrator to check on its status—only to learn my manager had pinged her two days earlier and told her to assign it to himself.

When I confronted my manager on a call, his response was almost laughable:

"You're not paying attention. You didn't even know this deal was in the books."

Of course I knew. That's why I caught it.

I escalated to HR. The deal was eventually returned to me. Neither of us deserved the bonus. But he deserved it less.

Then came the quiet annoyances. The kind you're expected to brush aside. Our office held a ping-pong tournament. I won—but only in the women's category. I'd played with the men in the office outside of competition. No one suggested I switch brackets.

I would've had more fun.

I reclaimed a sliver of dignity by tossing the cheap, made-in-China trophy straight into the trash. I wished I could've done the same with my work laptop. But the next morning, I was back in the office.

If they had a sense of humor, I rarely saw it. Or maybe it just didn't translate across cultures.

When it did surface, it was rare—and usually fell flat.

They never challenged authority, whether it came from a manager or a client. That wasn't just cultural—it was practical. Questioning power could cost you your job. Or your visa. Many were here on employer-sponsored visas. I was here as a U.S. citizen.

I talked about all this with my husband, but also—unexpectedly—with my mom. She had worked in a majority-Indian environment too, but her experience was completely different.

"They are diligent. Hardworking. Kind."
I saw those traits too. Why did I feel so miserable?
Then it hit me.

She worked in the real economy—the kind where diligence and cooperation produce something tangible. I worked in the Proximity Economy. At my job, most of the work was fake.

So what happens when diligence, discipline, and hard work can't lead to real output?

They morph into something else. Something less human. Americans were more comfortable with quiet quitting. Indians weren't. They wanted to work for it. But it wasn't just work ethic—it was culture, too. A tendency to hire their own. Rigid hierarchy. A reluctance to ask why.

When a faulty system meets a culture wired for compliance, something happens: the whole thing becomes stickier. More inert. More resistant to change.

With AI models, we became more productive—collectively. But some weren't comfortable with that. The work ethic was strong, but the instinct to perform the work was stronger. We met for the ritual of meeting.

I'd ask, "We already have the estimate. And the rationale. From ChatGPT. We all agree it's good enough. So... why the meeting?"

My manager would firmly respond: "Sarah, do you have something more important to work on?"

I didn't answer.

Everyone else was quiet.

Why did they hire me?

Because I was a customer-facing face. A white woman in leadership—someone who could connect with clients. Their leadership bench was thinner than what I'd seen at Mastercard or other firms, but it still looked very white.

I was a diversity hire. A presentation hire. They wanted more sale contracts—but they also needed to check a box. Mastercard had started asking all vendors about their diversity metrics before doing business. I was Mastercard's former employee.

I was the box.

Pandora's, probably—by the end of it.

They'd profile me in internal communications: What do I do outside of work? What's my horoscope? Who's my spirit animal? I wasn't sure—did they mean an actual animal, like an owl, or a celebrity, like Beyoncé? I gave them answers.

You can't stay in a system by embarrassing it. You embarrass yourself instead.

America, the great melting pot.

But some things just don't melt.

THE NEXT
GENERATION

HOW THEY BUILT THEM

A close friend—whom I'll later introduce as the Washington Insider—and I exchanged maybe twenty emails about Claudine Gay, Harvard's first Black president.

Before, during, and after her testimony.
Before, during, and after the backlash.
And then, after her resignation.

It was one of those stories that grabbed us both and wouldn't let go. It had everything: a prestigious downfall, a crisis of merit, public shaming, genuine regret, performative resignation.

He was thrilled by her downfall—barely able to contain his glee. That irritated me more than anything she said.

Which is probably why, by the end, I was fully on her side—even though her title, her power, and the institution she represented are core parts of the Proximity Economy. It's inner machinery.

I think we all instinctively side with the fallen—especially when someone else enjoys the takedown a little too much. Or maybe it was just a woman-for-woman thing.

She stumbled during her testimony—over words I don't think

she would have, if she hadn't been overthinking. Then she issued an apology:

"What I should have had the presence of mind to do in that moment was return to my guiding truth, which is that calls for violence against our Jewish community—threats to our Jewish students—have no place at Harvard and will never go unchallenged."

It felt genuine. And in my mind, that should have been enough. But there was some disdain. She ruffled too many feathers, I suppose. Everyone wanted accountability. Or maybe a few Harvard endowment sponsors made some calls. Larger politics at play.

Who knows. I can only speculate.

But she was forced out.

I don't know why, but I have a feeling this won't age well. It echoes how Monica Lewinsky was treated. Americans cringe now at how they treated her—how they missed the bigger picture.

How they ignored the system. Power dynamics.

My guess is, they'll feel the same one day about Claudine Gay.

I wanted her resignation letter to say something bolder, something closer to the real job description, as I imagine it:

> I don't know what people imagine this job entails, but here's my day-to-day: I talk to staff and students, attend fundraising events, meet with the board, and oversee an endowment fund larger than some countries' GDP. Harvard didn't hire me to upend the system. They hired me to preserve it.
>
> Universities are in the extraction business, just like corporations. But we don't extract from consumers—we extract from students.

We talk about education, inclusion, mobility, and opportunity, but what we really produce is the next generation trained to uphold credentialism, network effects, and corporate gatekeeping.

Yes, we have the most Nobel Prize winners.

We produce visionaries.

But we also supply corporations with a steady stream of followers.

They don't ask too many questions.

They follow rules. They follow authority.

They come from homes where parents teach them wealth preservation and incrementalism.

Then we take over. We are all about tradition, so we ingrain it in them—a necessary component for status quo preservation. Then we hand them over to you. Your corporate culture reinforces everything in practice. You teach them how to navigate hierarchies; we teach them how to signal innovation and leadership—how to speak the language of dynamism without disrupting anything.

Between the two of us, we shape the next generation. It's a symbiotic relationship—like politicians and lobbyists.

The education we sell? You can get most of it for free online.

Our tax-exempt status may have once been justified—when we were driving real innovation. But the golden age of discovery is long gone. What's left is credentialism—an expensive filter that reinforces status and stifles society more than it helps.

But she didn't say that.

She took the "high road."

She upheld the system.

And most of the time, that's what we choose—even when we're on our way out.

She looked weak—unfit for the role, even in an institution losing status by the day.

Washington Insider didn't email about it after her resignation.

No thoughts. No reaction. Just a link to the news.

We kept emailing, just not about her.

Maybe he sensed the win felt hollow by the end.

More likely, he poured champagne.

HOW WE FAIL THEM

've watched the system gradually reshape younger employees. They arrive with wide eyes and fresh enthusiasm, still carrying the hope instilled by graduation speeches urging them to "change the world." But the system dulls that spark fast. And once the paychecks start coming, something shifts—not just in them, but in us.

Their salaries free us from guilt. Once they're paid, we stop seeing them as kids. But often, they still are—creative, eager, naive. We stop feeling responsible for their disillusionment. After all, they're adults now, right? They're getting paid.

We assign vague projects, create false expectations, speak in corporate jargon, and ask them to "brainstorm solutions."

We tangle them in fluff—like Mother Gothel wrapping Rapunzel in her hair, singing "Mother knows best."

It's betrayal.

The generation that's leaving is betraying the one that's coming. Parents betraying their kids. Grandparents betraying their grandkids.

They say youth is wasted on the young, but maybe that's on us more than them.

Yes, there were opportunities to learn—for those curious enough to study the inherited digital machinery, to trace the anatomy of the Switch, to understand how the system perpetuates itself.

The younger employees had this energy—the best kind. A raw eagerness to feel useful. But also a quiet desperation to justify their paychecks. And yet, the system doesn't allow for blunt honesty—we can't just say, *There's nothing to do here—just learn to swim.* At the same time, you can't hold their hand for too long, because you're trying to stay afloat yourself.

They arrive wired for deadlines, conditioned by school to complete projects, essays, labs, and tests.

But here, there's no clear endpoint. No finite delivery.

Expectations are vague. They're simply expected to perform magic.

We don't need hard work or smarts.

We need abracadabra.

It's a recipe for quiet anxiety.

We were building the Network of the Future. That's what the project was called, anyway. A name like that sets huge expectations. How do you tell them it most likely won't become anything at all?

I'd try to reassure them: "Relax. The Switch is here. It'll keep providing—like Adam Smith's invisible hand at work."

But of course, they didn't trust me.

How could they?

They were still eager. Still convinced they were here to build something real.

They wanted to create the future.

But the past is the future. And the past has already been created.

We don't work with the past.

The past lives inside the omnipotent machine in the data center.

We work with abstraction—the image of what we think the machine is. What it could be.

Like in a movie, with holographic touchscreens and floating diagrams, we swipe and reshuffle screens, data, and components, trying to create a new abstraction out of old ones.

That's our job.

I remember one young woman who arrived straight from college. She was anxious at first but quickly found her survival strategy.

Technical skills weren't her strength, which made it hard to perform the magic that was expected. So she leaned into what she knew best, being visible, being present, being perceived as essential. She organized Cinco de Mayo celebrations, Latin American meet-and-greet groups, volunteering initiatives, and cultural events. Unlike the rest of us who worked remotely, she was more often in the office, present in every meeting, upbeat, engaged. She aligned with a more technical team, becoming symbolically productive by association.

Over time, she picked up just enough technical language to compliment others on their work and showed eager deference to the manager who had hired her. She took the influencer playbook, leveraging personal branding, engagement, and relentless visibility—and adapted it to corporate life.

And it worked. She lasted.

Leadership was filled with retirement-ready mid-level managers—many at Mastercard for over thirty years, some who had never worked anywhere else. They didn't even have LinkedIn profiles.

They didn't need to signal. Their entrenchment was the signal: I'm an expert. I'm loyal. I'm a leader. I value privacy. I'm too busy to market myself—everyone who matters already knows me.

A few had grown up on farms or in traditional Midwest communities, where hard work was a way of life.

They often grumbled about the younger generation, claiming they "did nothing." That was how they signaled they were still relevant. Or maybe it was just their own frustration with growing obsolescence, thinly disguised as nostalgia for a better work ethic.

All the while, the younger generation *was* trying to do something— but there was nothing to do. Leadership pointed to the future, and the flock followed, looking to us, the senior architects, for guidance.

"How do we get there?" their eyes asked.

And it was on us to show them. Not how to build. Not how to create.

But how to signal.

FIVE FRIENDS,
FIVE UNIVERSES

CLOSEST FRIENDS

t's life. Circumstances. Randomness.

All my closest friends are men—a radiology technician, an Amazon delivery driver, a teacher, a software engineer, and a Washington insider.

The kind who testifies before Congress and shakes hands with senators.

I never managed to find—or keep—a female best friend. I don't know if I was ever truly looking.

I would like to have one.

But even if I never do, life gave me two daughters and two sisters.

Maybe that evens things out.

I hold my male friends close.

But not all friendships survive the truth.

THE RADIOLOGY TECHNICIAN

The radiology technician has a sharp, dry humor that makes you wish you were quicker on your feet. His jokes hit with a precision that makes the obvious suddenly visible—something everyone only recognizes once it's said.

When he visits, he walks in and, if he notices the kids, says, "Oh, your kids still live here? Haven't moved out yet?"

Now that I've been around more, not flying off for work, he grins: "So, how's life as a housewife?"

Then he turns to my husband:

"And you? How's life as the main breadwinner?"

They both look at me, waiting.

I probably still hate those labels.

But I love his jokes.

We both love clean lines, crisp architecture, and evocative melodies. If the world had more stability, more harmony—we'd feel it instantly. He has an eye for hidden gems—mid-century homes tucked into the woods, old car parts, secondhand finds waiting to be restored. He sends me a listing for leftover high-performance glass panels—insulated, low-E, and a steal.

"Don't ask why. But you need these for the project you didn't know you had."

Every year for my birthday, he renews my Dwell subscription with a smirk. "Your blueprint for life," he calls it.

But he notices details I overlook—nuance in spaces, in music, in the way light hits a room at a certain time of day. He'll talk about a typeface or a new color for a kitchen wall, breaking down exactly why it works.

He's always fixing something on his mid-'90s burgundy Corrado. He takes me to car shows, but he can't afford a new car. When I point that out, he just smirks.

"I like to see what I'll be driving twenty years from now."

But that's just his side project. His real work takes up most of his time. He pulls long shifts at the hospital, his job keeping him in close proximity to suffering. People come to him for X-rays, often scared, sometimes in serious pain. He has to position them just right. A sixteen-year-old with a medial shift of the brain after a car crash—her family doesn't know yet. A one-month-old with a tumor—the family doesn't know yet.

A kid walks in for a scan, and he catches himself thinking, Please don't have cancer. Please don't have a tumor. The wait for the scanner to finish can be nerve-wracking. It's a daily occurrence. He sees what's wrong first.

A patient asks, "So how does it look?"

He already knows.

But all he says is, "Your doctor will go over the results."

I know how much he makes—he told me once.

I couldn't tell him his whole annual salary is my end-of-year bonus. He spends his days seeing sick babies, broken limbs, birth deformities, terminal diagnoses. He positions them for X-rays, holds them steady, absorbs the weight of their pain without showing it. Some technologist reading this is probably thinking: *All of this can be automated—even the poker face.*

I don't see suffering in my work. My professional life exists at a distance from anything truly human. He, on the other hand, faces it every day.

When we talk, I ask about his job—not just the technical parts, but the people. The hardest cases, the ones that stayed with him. I think it's because I wonder what it's like to be that close to pain.

I've experienced strangely little personal loss. I don't think I've ever even been to a funeral. It's weird. My grandparents passed away, and my uncle was killed in the war, but I was on another continent when it happened. My parents are alive. My closest friends are alive. My large extended family is alive. It feels almost unnatural—like I've been spared something fundamental.

I know loss is coming for me.

I have no idea if I'll know how to carry it when it does.

I hope I will.

If we learn through exposure, maybe not.

But if it's wired into us—maybe I'll manage.

He's reminded daily how quickly things can change. I imagine he comes home from work and hugs his child longer than I hug mine. Maybe he holds his wife closer.

His job doesn't allow detachment. Mine is built on it.

One night, we sat on his back patio, talking late into the evening. The conversation drifts from work to the economy to automation.

He wonders aloud if AI will take over his job.

"I think your job is safe," I tell him.

The machines might replace radiologists, but not him—not the human positioning the patient, adjusting for pain, comforting a child who's scared of the big, humming scanner.

But later, I realized I don't know. Maybe they will. Maybe, in the end, human proximity to suffering will be one more thing we delegate to machines.

THE AMAZON DRIVER

The Amazon driver splits his time between two lives—one for working, one for wandering. Both are living. Just differently. Half the year, he's in St. Louis, living with his brother's family. The arrangement works. His brother's wife jokes that the house came with a built-in babysitter. While in St. Louis, he freelances with Amazon Flex. The other half, he's in the Philippines or South America—living cheaply, eating well, parked in some beachside town, surrounded by others who've opted out of the work-and-die track. Abroad, he picks up side gigs on Upwork—web design, SEO[20] freelancing—just enough to stretch that freedom a little further.

For him, price decides everything. If a burger costs more than $10, he knows he's in a tourist trap—and he's already moving on.

It appears he's hacked the system in a way most people haven't: budget travel and the gig economy. I can see how, on the surface, they offer a strange kind of freedom—if you can stomach the trade-offs.

I tell him I think travel is overrated.

Philosopher Agnes Callard once made a solid case: "travel turns us into the worst version of ourselves while convincing us that we are

---

20. Search Engine Optimization (SEO): The practice of improving a website's visibility in search engine results to attract more traffic.

at our best." I think she's right. Some of the biggest arguments I've
had with my husband were during family trips. Maybe it's spending
money outside the normal budget—combined with high expectations. Everyone's just a little more sensitive, a little less patient. Add
to that all the free time, and comfort, and other people serving you—
of course we feel mildly miserable.

But he just shakes his head. It's not something he experiences;
he travels alone. Says it's the one thing that still makes him feel free.

When he's not traveling, he likes to work. He enjoys parts of his
job. Cold outside, warm in the car, coffee in hand, podcast playing—
it's a rhythm he knows. He doesn't work full days. On good days,
he can make $200 in three hours. He picks his rides. Knows which
blocks are worth his time. Some days, he does well. Other days, the
money's not worth it.

He's competing, he suspects, with undocumented immigrants.
He sees them camped out in parking lots, juggling two phones—
one their own, the other probably borrowed from someone with
legal status.

When too many drivers flood the system, the algorithm adjusts
the pay downward. And then there are the irrational ones—drivers
who take a $60 block that lasts three hours and, after gas and wear,
end up with just a few bucks an hour. He doesn't get it. But they
take it anyway.

I wonder about that.

Maybe they're poor. Maybe they're uneducated, undocumented,
unhoused.

And maybe they're irrational. Their bodies perform the work—
getting dressed, taking rides, navigating streets—while their minds
run on autopilot or muscle memory. Enabled just enough to function

but limited in ways that prevent them from performing simple cost-benefit analysis.

Economists like to assume rational consumer behavior. But how many people fall through the cracks simply because they're not? And shouldn't someone be catching them? Helping them? An algorithm, at least—if not another human.

His brother, a radiology technician, follows a more traditional trajectory: stable job, mortgage, predictable career path. But even he sees the appeal of the delivery driver's freedom. While he works long hours at the hospital, his brother is hopping islands in the Pacific, sharing photos of jungle hikes and street food feasts.

They both lift with the discipline of athletes. They look a decade younger than they are—but the genes are stacked against them. Recent bloodwork showed an ApoB level[21] over 190—dangerously high. Cardiovascular disease took most of the men on their father's side before they reached old age.

He feels like he's on borrowed time, so he spends as much of it as he can with his nephew—and lives like he's semi-retired.

We often circle back to bullshit jobs—it's a recurring theme in our conversations. He texts me from abroad: "I met a nineteen-year-old life coach in Vietnam today. Can you believe that? What kind of life advice can a nineteen-year-old give?"

It reminds me of other strange jobs I've read about. In China, a retail chain hired women to walk on treadmills so customers could see how clothes 'move.' In Japan, a man rents himself out to people who just need someone to do nothing with. Another guy charges boyfriends to beat him up in front of their girlfriends, so they can

---

21. ApoB is a protein tied to LDL particles—high levels mean more cholesterol traffic and higher heart disease risk.

feel protective. But at least those jobs—absurd as they are—don't pretend to be anything else. They're honest. All we need is a modern Chekhov to turn their tragedy and comedy into a play.

One night, we were at his brother's house, sitting on the patio. We are debating bullshit jobs, automation, and the state of work.

He's frustrated. He sees undocumented immigrants taking delivery jobs, pushing down wages, making it harder for people like him to earn a decent income in the one industry where effort matters.

I push back. "You're fighting over crumbs. The real money is in corporate America, in financial services, in tech. That's where the biggest slice of the economic pie is hoarded. The pie keeps growing—but the way it's sliced is completely broken."

He then tells me about his other gig—SEO and web design for an American company with offices in Bosnia. On his resume, he listed a Sarajevo address. He made it to the third interview. The employer liked him.

But he then casually mentioned he was a U.S. citizen who had a residence in St. Louis. That scared them off.

"They called me and said sorry, but we are looking exclusively for an offshore resource."

He clarified—he could work from Sarajevo, he's a dual citizen, he was genuinely interested in the role. But it was too late. He's rare in that he's felt both ends of the squeeze—undocumented workers pushing down wages in his driving gig, and an American tech company shutting him out through offshoring, even when he was willing to work abroad, just for being a U.S. citizen. It's the kind of thing that helps explain why Trump won.

The conversation stretches late into the night. A porch light flickers on. We've been talking too loudly—we might have woken up some neighbors.

On the drive home, I think about how proximity shapes perspective. He feels the impact of immigrants because they're in his immediate space, competing with him. I see corporations using inherited systems to extract value, rewarding those who maintain the illusion of productivity.

It's hard to share this kind of knowledge over one evening on the porch. You must be in the system to really understand it. Or write a whole book about it—and even then, maybe.

But I do wonder: when Amazon replaces him with drones, and the last crumbs disappear—what then?

THE TEACHER

The Teacher—my brother-in-law—lives in the world of ideas. He teaches in Chicago Public Schools. His apartment is a shrine to books and classical music.

When he first arrived in Texas at twenty-four—five years after I did—he didn't speak much English. I suggested ESL classes. Instead, he started with a Russian theologian and an Austrian composer. He read Alexander Schmemann's *For the Life of the World*. Later, he picked up a biography of Gustav Mahler written by his student, Bruno Walter. Like him, both Walter and Schmemann were immigrants to this country—one escaping Nazism, the other Bolshevism.

I wonder now if choosing those books was an escape from the new world into the old—or just the old world following him into the new.

When they were just dating, his now-wife likes to tell a story: one day she spotted his Amazon account open on her computer. The endless list of books—on history, philosophy, religion—along with stacks of classical music CDs he had purchased or saved to his wish list. Nothing practical. Nothing profane.

His purchase history didn't explain everything—but it made her pause. He was odd. But maybe in a healthy way.

Now, they have three small kids who fill their home with chaos and joy. When the screaming peaks, he puts on Ligeti's 10 Pieces for Wind Quintet.

He says, "It doesn't quiet the domestic noise. It just overwhelms it." The Teacher has always been like this.

While the rest of us got caught up in the usual distractions, he was different. He never cared to read, watch, or want what everyone else did.

A child of working-class parents in Bosnia, his childhood was interrupted by war. And yet, he emerged with a broad, encyclopedic knowledge of geography, history, and art—along with a growing affinity for the finer things in life. It didn't add up. And there was no explaining it.

By his teens, he was reading Dostoevsky, Andrić, Tolstoy, and Thomas Mann. We both love *The Magic Mountain*—maybe because we grew up on one. Our refugee camp, where we met as kids, was an old hotel, perched on a mountain, far from urban life. There was even an old lung sanatorium nearby at Iriški Venac. Reading the book there felt natural.

His ability to tune out the noise and focus on what truly matters has always been remarkable.

His wife tells a story about walking through Chicago with him one day, passing a man wearing an Air Jordan shirt with a prominent Nike logo. The Teacher noticed it and casually remarked, "Oh, that guy must work for Jordan Airlines."

But he teaches in high school and works with teenagers. Don't his students wear Nike? He later admitted he probably had seen it. But in that moment, *Jordan*—an airline, a country, some long-ago reference stored deeper in his mind—took over. That's how his brain works: a little misaligned with the common world.

Once, while driving downtown, they passed a street sign with a big crossed-out P above the words:

NO STOPPING
NO STANDING.

The street was empty.

He read it aloud, then asked, "Does that mean there's no parking?"

But ask him about the Russian Revolution, and he can talk for hours.

Sometimes I wonder if his kind of mind—curious to the point of being mildly unfit for modern life—is exactly what the future needs. When automation strips away the routines, only the curious will know what to do with the freedom.

Andrew Patner, a well-known Chicago-based classical music broadcaster, cultural critic, and a boulevardier, met him by accident at the Chicago Symphony Store, where my brother-in-law was working as a cashier, selling CDs. Andrew asked him something logistical—not realizing he was speaking to a like-minded enthusiast of classical music. A conversation started. Then another. And another.

On the surface, they couldn't have been more different. Andrew was an openly gay, Jewish, urban intellectual; my brother-in-law, a 6'7" socially conservative Orthodox Serb, twenty years younger, a former refugee. But they had so much in common. Their conversations spanned history, music, philosophy—an intellectual friendship that transcended every obvious divide.

Andrew invited him onto his radio show, where they discussed Byzantine music, chants, and other themes most of us wouldn't even think to explore. They became close, and he became a regular guest at our family's *slava*—the Serbian Orthodox patron saint's feast day. We all loved Andrew.

His passing was a deep loss—for the Teacher, and unexpectedly, for me. He had written the recommendations for my master's program in D.C.—and I got in. That small gesture helped shape my path. The ripples of his influence stretched further than he probably ever realized.

Over time, my brother-in-law transitioned into teaching. He teaches in a magnet school on the far West Side of Chicago, the area marked with decades of disinvestment and violence. He's an active member of the Chicago teachers' union. It's hard work—not just long, but heavy. The kind that follows you home. He loses students to shootings. It's rare—but it happens.

I get a text from his wife: *Call him. Bad day at school.*

He experiences tragedy, but he does his job with passion. It's exhausting and challenging, especially in the era of TikTok and You-Tube shorts.

Over the years, students compared him to NBA players. First Toni Kukoč, later Pau Gasol—and sometimes Abraham Lincoln, for his height and gaunt figure. He feels the weight of responsibility. He believes his job matters. He hopes it makes a difference.

"I still believe in the future of humanistic education, even though I have my doubts. Honestly, grades and numbers often feel inflated, and there's politics in the system. But real learning still happens—even if sometimes in a smaller percentage than I'd like."

Just driving from one end of Chicago to another can feel like crossing between different worlds.

He lives on the North Side but teaches on the West Side.

In one zip code, life expectancy is eighty-five. In another, it's barely sixty.

The gaps—they persist.

Zip codes as invisible borders.

The Teacher and I knew about borders long before we came to America. We just didn't know how deep they ran.

THE SOFTWARE ENGINEER

The Software Engineer is the brother of the Teacher. He doesn't think much about his job—whether it's useful or not. He's there for the paycheck. He's been working from his home office for over a decade.

He has been like that since we first arrived in America. He worked while I went to school, supporting me through my studies. Then it was my turn—I worked while he earned his degree.

Our life decisions have always been a shared journey, though he's been the one to say yes to everything.

"Do you want to go to America?" Yes.

"Should we get married? It might help with the U.S. embassy and our refugee application." Sure.

"We should move to Chicago." Sure.

"Let's have kids." Okay.

"How about D.C.?" Okay.

"Portland, OR?" Sure.

"Now St. Louis?" Sure.

"Your daughter wants an eyelash curler." Okay.

"Do you even know what that is?" No. But I'll figure it out.

He's my husband of twenty-six years. And, of course, he's my best friend.

I don't know if our marriage lasted this long because I am the way I am, or because he is the way he is.

We've both worked in IT for years, so we share a common language—not just the one shaped by industry, but a private one of silent categories and unspoken qualifications.

He recently got a new manager. He doesn't like him. I sometimes overhear their one-on-one meetings. Each call feels like an insult to intelligence. My husband's strategy is to distract his manager with questions he already knows the answers to—then walk him through the latest abstraction he built: usually a new or enhanced Splunk dashboard. If he doesn't do that, the manager starts with, "Let's see what we can find you to do so you can shine in the next customer meeting." For my husband, it's painful to listen to that—because the manager just joined the company. For me, it's painful, period.

We've worked under all kinds of managers. Over time, we started categorizing them.

"What type is he?" I ask.

"The worst," he says.

That's the kind who wants to work hard but doesn't have much to do, so he micromanages—but also desperately wants to be loved.

One afternoon, I was lying on the sofa, staring out the window, drained from another useless meeting. I started rambling about the meaninglessness of our work.

"My job isn't meaningless today," he said. "I just promoted code to production."

"What kind of code?" I asked. "What did you turn in?"

He explained: cybersecurity layers, app vulnerabilities. "A wall within a wall"—extra protection, logging, compliance tracking.

"But doesn't the OS already have a wall? And the network? And the database?" I asked. "How do you know your wall is even necessary? Has it ever stopped an actual attack?"

He looked at me, dead serious. "If I promote code to production, that means my job isn't useless."

"You're kidding, right? You think promoting code to production means your work matters?"

"Well, yeah," he said. "A lot of the time, I don't even get to promote it—the code gets scrapped in development or test. When it's promoted, it means it's finished, it works, and it's live."

It was one of those moments in marriage where you realize you live in parallel universes.

For him, getting code into production was proof. A task checked off. A concrete result. Done.

And I get it. There's something grounding about tangible work—if you don't stop to ask what it's really for.

"You need to follow the code," I said. "Where does it end up? What does it do?"

He thought about it.

Finally: "We have customers. Big banks. They need compliance audits."

He builds Splunk dashboards and reports that prove compliance. "The government audits them, so they need to show they're compliant," he explained.

It's not uncommon for these companies to lobby for the government to impose compliance rules that only they can verify.

I asked my husband if that might be the case. He doesn't know. And if he did, he wouldn't tell me.

He knows I'm writing a book. He's already worried it might cost him his job.

But from what I can tell, he's too far removed from the cause and effect—of the code, the business, the regulations. Not that he couldn't find out. If I had his job, I suspect I'd dig deeper. But he doesn't care.

It's interesting that he's so selective about what he consumes, but not at all selective about what he produces.

When he was shopping for a full-suspension mountain bike, he obsessed over every feature—aluminum vs. carbon frames, air vs. coil suspension, hydraulic vs. mechanical brakes.

But when it comes to the code he writes, he doesn't stop to ask where it goes or what it really does.

Shouldn't we care more about what we create than what we consume?

Does it really take the tortured soul of an artist to give a damn?

Balkan men never admit when you make a good point.

They don't concede. They don't argue. They don't even acknowledge they heard you.

They just sit with it.

Then, three weeks later, they'll repeat your point back to you—as if they thought of it themselves.

And that's how you know.

They agreed.

THE WASHINGTON INSIDER

The Washington Insider lives right next to the Capitol.

My other friendships are organic—rooted in years of shared history. With him, it feels constructed. We both know what good friendship should look like—like we studied the mechanics, aced the theory, and passed with an A+.

But every so often, I'll get an email from him and think—god, we don't actually know each other.

I think living in D.C. sharpened his manipulative side. When stakes feel high, everything—even the personal—turns transactional. I don't know if it's D.C., or just how we began—something we could never quite shift.

I wanted the friendship to be permanent, but I doubt it will be. Virtual friendships are projections—we invent each other.

He's married. Runs marathons. A friend who values nuance—he thinks before he answers and usually lands on: "It depends."

He is an economist. At one point, he juggled four jobs—one full-time, the others consulting, advisory, part-time.

Now he's planning what he calls "pretirement"—staying just busy enough to feel relevant, never burdened. Quiet quitting for the 50+ set.

We both live comfortable lives, though financially, he's in a different tier.

He's the one friend I can go to a great restaurant with without hesitation.

We can both afford it, but he usually pays—and it never feels awkward.

With him, there's no struggle. Reservations are made, calendars updated, nothing is left to chance.

His favorite saying is: "Those who fail to plan, plan to fail." I don't think it's just about how he works or lives. It feels deeper.

It's how he copes.

He has deep knowledge in one thing, but barely scratches the surface of most others—his curiosity stops at economics and politics.

No interest in the past—his, and even less mine.

No deeper sense of history, culture, or art.

No hobbies either, aside from some indulgences involving engines and the open road.

He often frames everything around happiness.

"Well, does it make you happy?"

"What makes you happy?"

I'm not sure what bothers me more—that he sees happiness as the ultimate goal, or that he assumes it must be everyone's, including mine.

Some people can step outside, feel the sun on their skin, and actually feel something.

I don't think I'm one of them—but he's even further removed.

He'll fly to Europe, climb mountains, spot an ibex in the wild—and all he'll say is: "It was cool."

He's a libertarian who votes Republican or Independent.

He's convinced DEI cost him jobs—that he was nominated but passed over because he wasn't the right demographic. Whether that's true or just perception doesn't really matter.

He resents any challenge to meritocracy and takes satisfaction in watching DEI unravel.

But DOGE? That's different. On that, he sides more with the Democrats.

He still laments government spending, true to his Republican leanings, but he doesn't approve of DOGE. That one hits closer. Too many friends and family are losing jobs.

Ten years ago, he was my professor. Back then, he wasn't just enthusiastic—he was into it. The most genuinely passionate professor I'd ever had.

He drilled into us the idea of opportunity costs and trade-offs—how to weigh choices, divide the pie, find balance.

Over the years, we stayed in touch.

I asked him for advice about further education.

At one point, I was naive enough to think a PhD in economics would be a worthwhile investment—of time, of money, of sanity.

He gave me terrible advice—he encouraged it. Even wrote a recommendation letter.

Luckily, WashU rejected my application.

He got me into running. I didn't run before I met him.

Then our paths crossed in Wisconsin.

He persuaded me to join him—and I never stopped.

After leaving teaching, he started looping me in on workplace tensions—mostly people problems.

I read his emails, tried to apply what I knew from my world to his.

I don't know if it helped. But he kept writing.

Maybe it just made him feel seen.

While most of my friends are raising kids or stepping back from work altogether, his world is built on maintaining connections and staying relevant.

His work isn't about productivity—it's about affiliations.

"I need to think about who I want to be associated with," he once wrote in an email.

The actual work? Panels, conferences, university lectures, light consulting, business travel.

"I've got a podcast, a few meetings, and a happy hour—should be a well-balanced day," he wrote.

One role demands about eight hours a month. "Not a heavy lift."

Another? "Mostly involves keeping my name on the masthead and showing up when needed."

He often frames his work in terms of policy impact.

"This project has the potential to change public policy for millions of Americans," he wrote.

But funding is always an uphill battle.

Later, he admitted they might be able to cobble together a third of the funding—not enough for a proper pilot. Now they were asking if it was even worth doing.

From "potential to change public policy for millions" to "not sure if it's worth doing"—all in a single email.

It's just like my job. Constant motion, occasional noise—but nothing that feels real.

During Trump's first term, he was nominated for a position. "I cleared the Committee," he said. But his name got lost in the shuffle of Washington deal-making.

Later, he mocked Kennedy Center board appointments as meaningless resume-builders— "They don't do anything," he said. And yet, he still wanted his own nomination to go through.

He hates the game but still wants to win it.

He occasionally sends me invites to panels and conferences where he speaks.

I joined a few times.

I watched people in suits, trading credentials, basking in the glow of their own relevance.

They're not elected, not even appointed.

They operate in a strange, well-funded space I still don't understand.

At one of his jobs, he once said they get funding from Google. Another time, Mastercard.

I still don't know what they think they're buying.

Eventually I told him: "Your fireside chats are just echo chambers."

I stopped logging in after that.

It was harsh, but he agreed.

He didn't get offended. Midwestern roots—kindness baked in.

One day he emailed about some work drama. I sensed it was wearing him down.

I replied: "Why not be a teacher?"

It's what Thomas More says to Richard in *A Man for All Seasons*— right before Richard chooses politics.

I almost added: *It profits a man nothing to give his soul for the whole world… but for Wales?*

But he wouldn't have gotten it. He's never seen it. We had different tastes in movies.

In another email, he mentioned his legacy.

I stared at the word, debating whether to call him out. Legacy. Does he really think any of it will be remembered?

He recently sent a bulleted update—four jobs, all orbiting the same struggles: the push and pull between management, employees, budgets, perceptions.

He asked what I thought.

I told him it's all performative—abstract, symbolic, bureaucratic. But still hyper-competitive—making it even worse.

He wrote back: "I agree with everything you said… I'm sorry you're still in a job where you don't have passion or feel like you're making a difference. I will say, even if I'm delusional, I feel like I'm making a difference."

There it was. He knows. But he needs to believe in it anyway.

Because if he lets go of that, what's left?

I wanted to shake him. *Face it, damn it. So I don't have to feel so alone.*

I know he genuinely wants to be useful. He doesn't want to be cynical. I don't want to be either—but circumstances led me there.

He doesn't have to quit his jobs. But he could admit what they are.

Because his world isn't so different from mine—what I am in corporate America, he is in D.C.

His wife is a federal employee and recently got a letter from DOGE—an option to quit her job and receive severance. But he's still holding on. Still collecting titles. Still staying in motion.

Slavoj Žižek uses a pointed metaphor for this kind of denial: *Wile E. Coyote* in the *Road Runner* cartoons. The Coyote races off a cliff but doesn't fall—not until he looks down and realizes there's nothing beneath him.

Žižek's point is that philosophy forces us to confront the void beneath our feet—the uncomfortable truths we'd rather ignore.

I think I'm the Coyote, and he's the Road Runner.

I looked down, so I fell.

He didn't, so he keeps running.

But there's no ground.

I see it even better now, from below.

If he reads this—and he will—he'll think it's unfair.

Maybe, for the first time, he'll feel what I sometimes felt with him: We don't actually know each other. He might think, not just that she didn't know me—but that she didn't seem like someone capable of this kind of betrayal.

I didn't name him. But I wrote it all down.

I did ask myself, is his comfort worth more than what this chapter does for the reader, for the book?

I chose the book over our friendship.

It was a choice.

I knew exactly what I was doing.

I chose betrayal.

THE WRITER

I've benefited from the system, played the system—and, fair's fair, been caught a few times for playing it too well.

Some days, I didn't even log in. No signals. No PTO. Why bother? It was all the same—just absence—until someone finally noticed.

My Washington Insider friend has connections, credentials, and financial security. He's testified before Congress, shaken hands with senators, spoken at think tanks, served on advisory boards. But he doesn't really influence anything. He's not pulling any levers. Power lives elsewhere.

He's an expert—but experts have slipped in popularity. Fauci put the last nail in the coffin, then gave the eulogy. These days, being an expert is almost a liability.

Congressional testimony is just performance—meant to look vetted, analyzed, legitimate. But the decisions are already made—by instinct, by party line, by pre-aligned interests. Like the rest of us, he's just a witness to the strategies, the moves, the whims of others.

He reminds me of Nemo, riding the back of a sea turtle—swept up in the current, not steering, just going along for the ride, feeding one particular echo chamber.

It's not just him.

My Amazon driver friend is constantly on the move—both literally and figuratively.

Working, traveling, checking boxes. Living like it's a race against time.

Before his father passed away, he asked him: *What makes you happy?*

His dad didn't have an answer right away. But eventually he did. A simple one: *I like working.*

He tells me now, "I think I'm the same way as my dad. I like working. I like doing something."

His dad left him a small vacation house on the Adriatic, on the Pelješac peninsula. That's where he spends a lot of time now—fixing things, building, home-improving. I imagine he'll retire there one day, enjoying the rugged beauty, the wine, the oysters and mussels. Still doing something. Just... quieter.

The radiology tech is different—his world is action too, but more hands-on, more local. His main job, then his side pursuits: hunting for mid-century gems on Facebook Marketplace, scavenging car parts in junkyards, fixing, restoring, making things useful again.

Yesterday, he sent me a photo of a pulley he hauled out of the junkyard, and some car seats he dug up. By the afternoon, the car seats were already installed in his car—like they'd always belonged there.

My husband is a software engineer. But that's not really what he's built for. He likes real things but works with abstractions. A people person who works with screens. He likes to move. But he sits. And even though his work ethic is remarkable, he lives with a quiet, constant fear of being let go.

I got him into this line of work. I graduated first, landed a well-paying job, and helped him transition into tech.

The Eve did its dirty deed—I offered him an apple, and he took it.

My only consolation is that he likes the money. So it's not a total mismatch.

My brother-in-law, the teacher—by contrast, finds meaning in reflection. He's steeped in books and music, teaching the next generation, building a quiet world of ideas. His movement is inward—through thought, through memory. He doesn't need to "progress" in the traditional sense. He works. He teaches. All he needs is time: time to read, to reflect, to be with his family, to honor his ancestors, to give thanks to God.

He is the only one with faith.

The rest of us have none.

Yet we live as if we're the ones clinging to the promise of Matthew 7:7: *Ask, and it shall be given you; seek, and ye shall find; knock, and it shall be opened unto you.*

We are the ones asking, seeking, knocking—not metaphorically, but literally.

He simply believes it will come.

I used to think I was just a different kind of mover. But writing this book makes me wonder—am I slowing down? Or simply shifting closer to the teacher, embracing reflection, trying to make sense of things rather than just doing.

But I don't have his faith.

And my curiosity—my intellectual pursuits—don't stretch as wide as his.

I have my parents' restless drive—my father always needing to do something, my mother refusing to retire. Stillness isn't in my nature.

A psychologist friend once floated that all that ambition, movement, drive—it's just unresolved trauma, lingering.

Maybe. What do I know.

But maybe there are still sins—mine or someone else's—waiting to surface.

A reason to keep watching.

A new pattern of signaling, a quirk of human psychology I'll wish I'd noticed sooner.

But why does it still feel like survival, even now, when some of the smartest people insist we're on the brink of an age of abundance—if not already living in it?

Keynes predicted that by now, technological progress would shrink the workweek to fifteen hours, freeing us for leisure, fulfillment, and play.

And for some, that future has arrived.

But the survival script is still running.

Maybe that's just human nature.

Maybe it's inertia.

And maybe it's greed.

THE CASE
FOR DOCE

DOGE FIXES
HALF THE PROBLEM

My husband is hooked on DOGE. He's been waiting for Washington's excesses to be reined in for years. He tracks Nancy Pelosi's stock picks—the best-performing portfolio in America, he jokes. Palantir alone gave him triple-digit returns. Not a fortune, but enough to make his case. He still shows me the numbers—half gloating, half vindicated.

Is it possible that behind every guy betting on meme stocks is a woman saying no?

We lived in D.C. for a couple of years while I was in grad school, and he stayed home with the kids. He hated it—the heat, the mosquitoes, the prices, the Washington elite. Nothing drained our savings faster than those D.C. years. He told our kids the city was home to the two worst species: mosquitoes and politicians. He drilled it into them.

"What are the two worst species in D.C.?" he'd ask.

"Mosquitoes and politicians!" they'd recite.

He'd beam with pride.

Nuance matters. But I don't interfere.

Congress—and the agencies created by each administration to "redefine" government, to make it more efficient—have mostly failed.

Even the people working inside federal agencies talk about it.

On the record, off the record—for years.

They live through the same dynamic I've experienced in the corporate world:

They start with, "What can I accomplish today?"

But they hit brick walls, complexity, bureaucracy.

Eventually, the question shifts: "What will look like a productive activity?"

What begins as a tactic—to appear busy—eventually becomes the default. They shift, like I did, from real work and outcomes to performance, hierarchy, and politics. When enough people do that, the system stalls. There's no waking it up. Reorgs don't work.

You need a reset.

You bring DOGE.

My husband sees it as a game—he's got his team.

I see it as a reckoning.

But I also tell him it's not enough. The rot and waste aren't just in government. It's in corporations too.

Corporate inefficiency hides in plain sight—wrapped in branding, shareholder loyalty, and the illusion of productivity.

I once watched a Mastercard executive quiz a new hire:

"Who's our biggest threat?"

"Visa," the hire answered.

"Wrong," he said. "It's regulators."

No kidding—a duopoly like Mastercard and Visa should have regulators breathing down their necks. But one glance at their balance sheets tells you how well that's going. Not that I said anything to the executive or the new hire. At Mastercard, you don't even say the word *duopoly*. It's considered rude.

Both governments and corporations are run by the same species—humans. Ambitious humans who protect and hoard their power. Pretending corporations are *'good'* and regulators are "bad" is a false narrative. Plenty of "for-profit" companies accumulate wealth more steadily and predictably than the government collects taxes.

People can vote with their feet—move to lower-tax areas. Some even cheat on their taxes. It's an option. But you can't cheat when higher prices are baked in—when merchants pass the fees they pay to banks and payment networks straight to consumers.

DOGE is just the beginning. The real reckoning is still ahead.

A TRILLION-DOLLAR ILLUSION

About ten years ago, I interviewed at McKinsey while dealing with iron-deficiency anemia.

My anemia was so bad I couldn't recall words, think straight, or walk ten minutes home without gasping for air. Some days, I had to call a cab just to cover a few blocks.

We lived in Portland, Oregon at the time. The prettiest city—but I got sucked into its vegan subculture.

While breastfeeding, no less.

I think it's the dumbest thing I've ever done. Not just nutritionally. Like ever.

Culture matters. Some cities can literally kill you.

By the time I got on the call, I was slurring my words—barely coherent, let alone ready for their infamous "How many windows are in New York City?" question. I didn't get that exact one, but I got something similar. Still, that's the one that stuck.

The point wasn't to get the right answer. It was about how you approached the problem—breaking it down into components, making assumptions, estimating logically. Residential, commercial, public spaces, car windows, subways. You calculate averages and land somewhere around 30 million windows.

Now I see the parallel: estimating NYC windows is like estimating the deadweight cost of one corner of the Proximity Economy—finance, fintech, consulting. Both rely on simplifications and assumptions.

A Single Company: Mastercard ~33,400 employees.

I start with the one I know best. Aligned with Proximity Economy role logic:

— System Gatekeepers (1%) → ~334 employees

   Executive and C-suite. High salaries, symbolic oversight. Some useful work.

   Excluded from wage waste calculations.

— Innovation Signalers & Noise Creators (70%) → ~23,380 employees

   SVP, VP, Directors, Principals, Senior Analysts.

   The largest group—responsible for pilots, frameworks, decks, and transformation theater.

   Included in wage waste calculations.

— Expansion Operators & Administrators (15%) → ~5,010 employees

   HR, compliance, onboarding, internal comms, form-driven client operations.

   Often doing something, but low salaries and mixed impact.

   Excluded from wage waste calculations.

— Maintenance Workers (5%) → ~1,670 employees

Data techs, network engineers, janitorial and cafeteria staff—largely invisible but essential.
The only consistently value-producing group so excluded from wage waste.

Other support staff (9%)—are excluded from wage waste calculations due to either low salaries or essential functions.

So, the conservative estimate for Non-Productive Roles is 70%. System Gatekeepers—high salaries but low in number—and Administrators—higher in number but modestly paid—are excluded for simplicity.

At Mastercard, the average cost of Innovation Signalers and Noise Creators—SVPs, VPs, Directors, Principals, Senior Analysts—landed around $200K. It's a tech company—salaries run high. And Mastercard is just one company. Scale this across industries, and the waste explodes.

Scaling Across Industries in the US.

If we assume similar proportions apply across other U.S.-based proximity sectors—finance, fintech, consulting—and conservatively apply the $200K average salary only to the 70% of roles that fit the Innovation Signaler and Noise Creator profile, the waste becomes systemic and staggering.

— Finance Industry (~7 million employees) → $1.4 trillion annually

— Fintech Industry (~250,000 employees) → $50 billion annually

— Consulting Industry (~1.8 million employees) →
$360 billion annually

Total Annual Deadweight Cost Across These U.S.
Industries: **$1.81 trillion**

And that's just three industries—and just within the U.S.

— The UN estimates that transitioning to a green economy
would require $1 trillion annually—this inefficiency could
fund that nearly twice

— It's over 10× the annual cost to end global poverty ($175B)

— It's enough to build three U.S. Interstate Highway Systems—each costing ~$535 billion (adjusted for inflation)

It's stupidity.
Pepper spray in our eyes.
Trillions wasted.

DOCE: NEXT STEP

Waste is quiet—until it isn't. And when it surfaces, it's almost satisfying.

"After a six-week review, we are officially canceling 83% of the programs at USAID."

That's Marco Rubio, Secretary of State.

"Most did not serve—and in some cases even harmed—the core national interests of the United States."

He thanked DOGE. I do too.

In Bosnia—my first home—USAID and the National Endowment for Democracy (NED) funneled money into media outlets, funding internet portals aimed at opposing democratically elected leaders. Why? Because a handful of Bosnian American lobbyists in D.C.—people I know personally—decided the mainstream media weren't doing enough to promote ethnic unity.

They're the kind of elitists I distrust most: detached, self-assured, performative—completely out of touch with the country's cultural and political reality.

So I was glad when the money stopped. It was doing more harm than good.

The cuts happening under DOGE follow a familiar pattern.

It looks like the Pareto Principle—the 80/20 rule—playing out again.

— USAID: Cut 80%, keep 20%.

— Twitter: Cut 80%, keep 20%.

— OldTech: Not there yet, but the same logic applies.

— BigTech: Maybe not quite 80/20, but close—maybe 50/50.

And who's going to do it? Not the FTC. Not the DOJ. Not the SEC.

They had their chance. They could've stopped the worst of private-sector extraction, but instead chased hard proof—and got tangled in their own inefficiencies. When they finally act, it's fines and settlements—nothing that truly disrupts the system.

The antitrust laws meant to curb corporate dominance are outdated, inadequate, and too weak to dismantle the Proximity Economy.

At Mastercard, mention the Durbin Amendment and people start shifting in their seats. Like a trauma that's still lurking—contained, but always ready to explode. It's a law passed in 2010, meant to cap debit card swipe fees and lower costs for consumers.

But what happened instead?

The people it was meant to help got screwed.

The law produced unintended consequences—not because it was a bad law, but because the financial sector found a way to readjust its positions.

If the Durbin Amendment had applied to credit cards—not just debit—it might have shifted the landscape.

But it didn't.

So banks hiked checking account fees. Retailers pocketed the savings. Networks shrugged.

Free checking vanished. The unbanked paid more.

And the ones it was written for paid the price.

We need DOCE. A new federal entity: the Department of Corporate Efficiency—DOCE.

Independent. Comprehensive. Algorithmically literate.

If DOGE cuts federal spending, DOCE cuts corporate inefficiency and extraction.

If DOGE takes down bureaucratic deadweight, DOCE takes down corporate deadweight.

If DOGE drains the swamp, DOCE breaks the Algorithmic Aristocracy.

Some will say DOCE will never happen. That it's a fantasy.

But the conditions that make it necessary are already here.

It doesn't have to start as an institution. It can start as a mindset.

DOGE started as a meme and became policy.

A lot of people don't like Elon Musk. I think he has good instincts, good intentions.

Almost everyone responds to his energy—that intensity, that appetite for disruption.

I imagine someone with his force—just pointed in the other direction—leading DOCE.

If DOGE is about draining the swamp, defending democracy, then DOCE would be about defending markets.

Not preserving them but cleaning them up. Clearing out the rot.

Fixing what's imperfect, extractive, unearned.

DOCE would expose the bloat.

It would calculate inefficiency scores.

Create live rankings.

Track where the revenue actually comes from.

Publish an Innovation Signaling Index—publicly.

And start with the worst offenders:

Visa, Mastercard, JPMorgan Chase, Wells Fargo, Goldman Sachs, Bank of America, Citigroup, Experian, Equifax.

Corporations already use AI to scan us—predicting agreeableness, extraversion, neuroticism—sorting us like cattle based on whatever pseudoscientific nonsense they can extract from a headshot.

Fine. Let's turn the mirror around.

Use real AI—scientific, grounded—to scan them the way they scan us.

Quantify how much of their so-called "innovation" is just smoke and mirrors. If their press releases are any clue: 100%.

Expose how much of their revenue comes not from progress but from inherited digital machinery and extraction.

They want to optimize us?

For what? For signaling.

DOCE needs to optimize them.

Yes, layoffs. As a goal, not a byproduct.

They can hit them with fines, sure. Maybe even layoffs will follow.

But fines are just patches.

These entities don't need a slap on the wrist. They need to be transformed.

The king must be naked—or we'll keep bowing to an illusion.

It's the unavoidable consequence of an economy where millions are paid to pretend to work.

Wall Street will call it "market turbulence." Maybe even a recession.

The rational observer will call it what it is: long-overdue layoffs finally hitting the Algorithmic Aristocracy.

And if a company is "too big to fail?"

Turn it into a public utility.

Visa and Mastercard already function as public utilities—just without the accountability. It's time they were treated as such.

They were built on inherited digital machinery—the Switch—created over fifty years ago. It's public infrastructure now.

Private ownership isn't just unnecessary—it's expired.

But they're just the tip of the iceberg.

Financial Gatekeepers: Experian, TransUnion, Equifax, FIS, Fiserv, PayPal, Stripe. They don't innovate; they extract.

Internet & Cloud Infrastructure: Equinix, Digital Realty, Cloudflare, Akamai. They own digital roads and charge tolls.

Logistics Monopolies: UPS, FedEx, Union Pacific, BNSF. Private profits, public dependence.

Healthcare & Identity Gatekeeping: Epic Systems, Cerner, UnitedHealth, ID.me, LexisNexis. They control access to health and identity, but not for public good.

These companies aren't just dominant—they're foundational. But they operate like extractors, not stewards.

Sounds like communism? No. Just state capacity. And history.

And if we're bold enough to "drain the swamp" in government, why are we afraid to drain it in the corporate world?

It's not communism. It's consistency.

To fix the system, we need DOCE—independent, data-driven, ruthless.

BE THE VIRUS

What else is there, besides DOCE? Not much.

The system is designed to make us feel small. Powerless. Like there's no way out.

There are some small cracks.

You can look for ways to buy and sell directly—to other humans. To real people. Not platforms.

Use cash when you can—it has its own issues, but it bypasses networks.

Support local businesses—not because it's cute, but because it's strategy.

If you're tech-savvy, explore stablecoins or open-source alternatives.

The blockchain isn't the answer to everything—but sometimes it's a tool. Sometimes it's leverage.

If nothing else, it shows us that public alternatives are possible.

So demand them. Like a central bank digital currency (CBDC).

Yes, it raises privacy concerns. But we're already giving up privacy—to banks, platforms.

The difference is, one is (at least in theory) accountable to the public. The others answer to shareholders.

I try not to be the patch to their system.

Patches fix holes. Viruses rewrite systems.

I try to be the virus.

And the best move?

Vote for someone—anyone—who has the guts to bring DOCE.

Not because it fixes everything. But because it starts something.

BEYOND PAYROLL

BORING STICKS AROUND

For a few months at the end of 2024, every two weeks, I was at PNC in Pittsburgh. The bank's history dates back to before the Civil War and the abolition of slavery. It's older than the country's labor rights, older than its banking regulations. It's that old. In 1852, it opened its first offices on Liberty Avenue and 12th Street. Nearly two centuries later, I walk the same avenue to work. I put my hand on some trees along the way.

Now, it's a glass tower—soaring, reflective, sleek. The lobby is vast, almost cavernous, stretching so high that the elevators must be split into zones. You don't just press a button; you select your destination on a touchscreen, and the system assigns you an elevator. Seamless, modern entry into the OldTech.

When I was onboarded as a client partner, the bank gave me a PNC laptop and a few free goodies—an orange piggy bank, a sticker that read "Boring" with the PNC logo encircled in the letter O, and another that said "Boring Sticks Around."

Clever.

They turned stagnation into branding.

Almost admirable in its honesty.

My job is relationships. But not just any relationships—C-suite relationships.

I work for Synechron—an Indian IT consulting company.

About 200 of its employees support the PNC account, most of them offshore. My boss brought me in to help build relationships with PNC's newly restructured female C-suite—a decision he mentioned casually, without much thought for how it might read in an HR memo. The assumption was that, as a woman in tech, I'd forge a more natural connection than my male counterparts from the offshore team. It's a win-win: he gets credit for hiring a woman, and it's supposed to be good for business. But things are rarely that simple.

I connected with a few women. But my first point of contact isn't the executives themselves but their assistants. First, I take the assistants to lunch and dinner. Then, if I navigate that well enough, I take their bosses.

In these meetings, I ask questions. I listen. I flatter egos. They're always rushing. The conversations are all about names, titles, and proximity to power. Knowing *who* is working on something matters more than knowing *whether* it's working.

I memorize the C-suite and their direct reports: first name, last name, organization.

I follow up with the Chief Security Officer, tell her I'm writing a book, ask if she'd be willing to contribute her unique leadership perspective. She replies—she's interested but needs approval from legal and comms first. Maybe that's corporate deep state.

But the real relationship I was meant to build was with the Head of Technology.

I "met" her only through the larger-than-life digital portrait in the lobby—a Dior-ad-worthy image of polished perfection. Pristine white clothing. Blow-dried hair. Hands delicately crossed. A gleaming manicure. She's not just presented as a leader, but as a symbol—carefully curated to represent progress and inclusion. At times, more brand than executive.

What does she think when she sees that towering image of herself as she waits for the elevators? Is she proud? Or does she think, *Oh geez*.

Does she realize she's been turned into a brand—her likeness repurposed into corporate messaging?

She sets the culture—appearing in all-hands meetings, repeating the script: innovation, digital transformation, inclusion. It's the same everywhere. Every leader in OldTech must craft the story, the narrative that moves. And they must coin the phrases that stick.

At PNC, they call it *customer obsessed*. Same old idea, new word. It's always been about the customer—service, experience, top priority.

Now they're just *obsessed*.

Next up? *Possessed*.

A boring bank that's customer-possessed.

I like that.

These slogans spread like wildfire. One exec says it, and suddenly the whole company repeats it—emails, town halls, LinkedIn humblebrags. Like Finding Nemo's seagulls: one squawks "Mine!" and the others follow— "Mine! Mine! Mine!" No pause, no thought. Just echo.

They tell her story like a modern fable: once a college student stretching a single meal across two snacks, now Head of Technology, champion of Low Cash Mode—a tool to help poor customers, like she once was, avoid overdraft fees.

A hero, solving a problem.

A problem the bank created in the first place.

The floor is completely empty. Not even a cleaning crew on site. Just me.

Some extend their weekends. Others stay fully remote.

My calendar offers gems like:

Join us on Tuesday for an informative session on "Healthy Smiles for Working Professionals." Dr. So-and-So, DDS, will discuss dental hygiene and its fundamental role in maintaining overall health.

Like we're five years old in a corporate daycare.

The desks and chairs look new—modern, untouched. All desks have a lifting feature.

Splashes of orange—their logo orange—trail across the furniture and walls.

There's a video I want to watch.

Across the street, a Beaux-Arts building glows in the afternoon light—lion heads, jaws open, like the opening shot of a movie. The only thing missing is the popcorn.

I open the corporate strategy video and hit play. A leader takes the stage—confident, well-spoken, impeccably suited, armed with nothing but a PowerPoint clicker.

The plan: 200 new branches in the South. A $1.5 billion bet on brick-and-mortar banking. In the age of digital banking.

Who even goes to a bank anymore? I go maybe once a year—if that. What do people do there? Withdraw cash fee-free? Chitchat? Maybe banks are turning into community centers. Free coffee, a friendly teller. Maybe it's not so bad.

Miami alone will get forty-one new branches.

I pull up a map. The city's already drowning in banks. Another 41? That's a branch on every corner.

Maybe Miamians can justify it—another branch, another place to pee. I check the policy. Restrooms, of course, are for customers only.

I know why they're doing it. The money is shifting south, and they're following it.

It's not about serving more people. It's about serving the right people. Deeper pockets, larger deposits, and fewer financial headaches.

None of this is growing the economic pie. Banks aren't expanding the pie. They're just reshuffling it.

Every new branch is funded by overdraft fees, interest spreads, and account charges—costs quietly pushed onto customers. Branches will close in the Northwest and Midwest, some in communities that need them more than the wealthy South.

Later in the presentation, a woman in a suit steps up to the podium. They boast about 364 new "core consumer features." The leader's favorite? A texting feature to notify customers when their online banking is up or down.

Another alert, another algorithmic attention rent, in a world already drowning in notifications.

But 364? Of what? One for every day of the year?

2024 was a leap year. So, naturally, we got *only* 364 more things to click.

It's not innovation. It's a manager justifying a budget—a big number to signal work, progress—or the illusion of both.

I open the PNC bank app.

I count the features—and don't even find fifty.

Behind a number like that, there has to be some KPI invented to quantify success.

And once it exists, the numbers have to keep going up.

Year 1: Something reasonable—maybe twenty consumer features.

Year N: 364

They're just padding numbers to justify jobs and budgets.

I suspect it's the same in Congress. They pass a budget.

Year 1: Something reasonable.

Year N: Billions.

A few days later, my manager calls.

He's heard from PNC that I'm writing a book. The world is small.

"Is the book real, or just a way to get to the C-suite?"

"It's real," I say.

I tell him it's critical of the financial industry. A moment of honesty that unsettles him.

It lingers.

Two days later, he calls again.

"I've been thinking about our conversation. About your book. Why would you write a book criticizing financial institutions when those are our clients?"

It's the kind of thing many managers think, but few actually say out loud. The honesty was almost refreshing—until it wasn't.

Then he asks me to resign.

It's December 11th, 2024.

"Gladly," I say. "After the holidays."

THE FREE FALL

adjust my story depending on who I'm talking to, shaping it to fit their view of the world—their understanding of work.

It's just this book for six months," I tell my family. "Then I'll go back to work. I'll look for a new job." That's what I say, anyway.

I'm easing them into a new reality. Where I come from, being out of work isn't just personal—it unsettles everyone. In the Balkans, status still matters. So does shame. We leaned on each other more—especially during socialism. I don't know if we chose socialism because we were collectivist, or became collectivist because we chose socialism. Either way, that wiring lingers. Even now, with free markets and rising individualism, the need for approval hasn't fully let go. And it goes both ways. I care what people think. But they care what I do.

We don't really do *mind your own business.*

To my dad, I say:

"I've worked since I was eighteen. I didn't even take time off when I had the girls—except for eight weeks of paid maternity leave. I need six months for myself."

He hesitates, then nods. "Six months. Okay, I suppose."

Then the real question:

"But will you be able to find another job?"

"Of course I will," I say. "I'm a Subject Matter Expert. A SME. I have unique knowledge that nobody else has."

He exhales, finally somewhat relieved. I know what he needs to hear.

My daughters are worried about clothes and shopping.

"Will we have to go to thrift stores? Tina's got Dos in Chesterfield—she keeps gently preowned lululemon. Nobody will know."

My husband is on board with the book—but not so sure about his job. His employer just did another round of layoffs. "They flattened the hierarchy," he told me. "It's flat like a pancake now."

His manager has no other managers left to talk to, so now he talks to him and others in R&D about profit and loss—something they never had to care about before. On his last call, he sounded strange.

"Do you have enough things to work on until June?" his manager asked.

My husband hung up and said, "June? Why June? Why would he ask me that?"

My mom likes the idea but is surprised I'm the one writing it.

"I always thought your sister would be the one writing a book. Her life is more interesting."

My younger sister lives alone on a sailboat near the Statue of Liberty. She teaches at a Christian school and lives completely off-grid—wind for motion, solar panels for power, a dinghy or scooter to get around. She chose a life of service—to people, to God, to the environment. She read a few sections.

"Oh wow," she said. "Is this what you sinners are going through?"

My youngest sister in Milwaukee has six kids. She's too busy to think about anything beyond what's immediately in front of her. Even when I think about her, I hesitate to call her. We text. Mostly logistics.

My friends wondered if I could just do it on the side— "like a hobby."

The Washington Insider read a few sections. Unlike the others, he didn't ask why I wasn't working. He just said, "I'm glad you're fully into your writing project. I think it's shaping up well. You've got something there."

I have savings—I could have saved more—but I'd had a good income for twenty years and built myself a Fuck You Position (as John Goodman so deliciously put it in *The Gambler*).[22]

A Fuck You Position only extends your lifestyle beyond the job. You sleep well. But it doesn't protect your sense of self.

That inertia lasts much longer.

"What do you do?" The answer defines you.

I had a hair appointment the other day. The stylist asked me that very question.

"What do you do?"

For a moment, I wondered if I should tell her about my Airbnbs. The book. The kids.

I wanted to see how it felt.

I looked at myself in the mirror and said,

"I'm unemployed."

It felt OK. I didn't disappear.

But then she raised her eyebrows, just slightly.

"Oh... what did you do before?"

"I was an architect. Not of buildings—of technology," I lie.

I was a Nothing Person.

But I don't say that.

---

22. The "Fuck You Position" comes from a scene in *The Gambler* (2014), where John Goodman's character, a loan shark, explains to Mark Wahlberg's character that the only real freedom in life comes from having enough money to say "fuck you" to anyone. It's not about wealth for its own sake—it's about leverage, insulation from need, and the ability to walk away.

THE CLOSED LOOP

bought myself six months. But then what?

After leaving my last job, I didn't flip my LinkedIn profile to "Open to Work." I've seen former coworkers leave theirs up too long—stuck in professional limbo. I don't even want to know.

If there's a financial collapse, some kind of forced return, could I go back? Could I walk into another interview and act excited?

I doubt it.

My demeanor will give me away.

She looks like she'll do it her way, not ours.

Pass.

Some days, it feels like the realization is spreading—

that there's a kind of fakery seeping out of the corporate world.

Like there's a curtain before you even step into the lobby.

And it's about to fall.

Maybe it won't even be my decision.

I'll just get swept along with the rest—caught in the current.

Recession. Automation. Skill obsolescence. AI.

Maybe that's what saves me.

From having to explain why six months...

turned into more.

But I also have doubts about AI.
    That it's as effective as people say.
    That it's anything more than a mirror.
    Will it automate useless jobs?
    Will the bots just mimic what we did—
    The same performance, but with code?
    Nothing Bots. Nothing Agents.
    We'll find out, I guess.
    Or maybe we won't.

Tyler Cowen says that as AI spreads, the one skill that will matter most is networking: "Build your network, invest in relationships, work with great peers and mentors at all levels, and you'll be fine."

The network?! I scroll through my LinkedIn connections—600+ strong. Not random adds. I've crossed paths with them over 20 years in the field. But who are these people? I have no idea. Maybe I know 10 well. 20 at most. I have no network. Not one that would save me.

If I'd spent years massaging that network of Nothing People, I'd have no real life to remember.

I think I've worked for every bank in the U.S., in a consulting capacity. Not the community banks, of course. But if it's got a recognizable name, I've probably been there.

When I was at Accenture, before Mastercard, I traveled constantly. Sometimes just a month at a client. Then a new one. Another city. Another hotel. Same job, new people.

In fact, when I got the job at Mastercard, I didn't even realize I'd worked there before. Only when I showed up on campus did it hit me—wait, I think I've been here.

Two weeks later, a familiar coworker confirms it.

"You've worked here before."

"I thought I did," I say. "What did I do?"

"IBM sent you. You created a BIRT stored procedure for one Maximo report."

"Oh. Yeah. That sounds like something I would've done."

"You kept mispronouncing O'Fallon. You said it like it was French—*Oh-fah-LOHN.*"

"I still pronounce it that way. What's the proper way?"

"It's *Oh-FAL-en.*"

Gotta love the Midwest.

How do I know only 20 people? I should know more. But I don't. That's just how it is.

I've touched so many players, left no mark. Worse—I sometimes announced it: *Look, there is no mark.*

You're not supposed to say that. Ever.

And the few people I do know? The ones I occasionally check in on? The ones who might vouch for me, maybe even hire me? They have "Open to Work" banners themselves.

Maybe networking works for some people.

But not for me.

It's a closed loop—a game designed for those already inside.

And I stepped out. Six months, maybe more.

Which means I'm not inside anymore.

Not just not inside.

I'm not up.

I'm down.

Looking up.

Damn it—I've fallen. And as I fell, the rewards—

They slipped with me—
Caught in the nets of those still up there.
Still inside.
They didn't even notice.
They're too busy mining the Switch.

THE FIGHT
TO STAY HUMAN

CURATED STRUGGLE

Machines now rival PhDs—and will soon exceed them. There's nowhere left to climb. No higher credential to chase. The market has hit a ceiling.

How will we decide who gets the rewards the machines generate?

Tyler Cowen was asked recently about the jobs of the future.

He co-wrote a book called *Talent*—a kind of scouting guide for Silicon Valley elites. It reads like a manual on how to spot, assess, woo, and retain the highly gifted. The book treats talent like a scarce resource—elite capital to be identified and acquired. It's not written for regular people. It's written for those who think they'll be in charge of deciding who matters next.

When asked what kinds of jobs will remain in the age of AI, he answered:

"Jobs will go to those who can network—and those who can be human."

Networking is a closed loop. If you're in, you're in.

So what about the other half?

Those who can be human?

If all it takes is being human and having a network, then meritocracy's already dead.

We're all human. And networking just means you were already inside.

I'm simplifying, but patterns are emerging—and they point to where things might be headed.

If jobs now go to humans, then the credential chase is over.

Maybe I can stop saving for kids' college.

There are cheaper ways to get educated. A degree was always just a ticket to a job anyway.

Now that jobs go to the human, we're good. They're already human.

Some will be hired for their humanity. The rest nudged onto UBI.

Then the roles will rotate—those on UBI brought back in to work, while the others step out. A kind of distribution cycle.

Problem solved.

But why would Cowen say it that way—"Jobs will go to those who can network—and those who can be human"?

What if we still need a story about deservingness, even when the machines are doing all the work?

And I don't mean in the real economy—where goods are made, things are built, people are fed.

I'm talking about the Proximity Economy.

We still crave a moral framework.

We still want to believe people earned their spot.

What if our puritanical attachment to traditional work—our discomfort with unearned security, with safety nets—gets in the way?

Maybe we'll still demand a performance of effort. A performance of humanness.

Not because it's necessary, but because it *feels* fair.

What if we can't let go of the idea that everyone is equally human?

What if the market decides to adapt?

It makes a U-turn. Since it can't climb higher than the PhD to sort us out, it pivots back to something older, murkier.

Something primal.

What if some of us are *more human*?

Like—real. Raw. Human. *Originale.*

What kind of humans would be more human than the rest?

It would be the ones who can demonstrate struggle. Sacrifice. Grit. The appearance of empathy.

The things machines can't fake.

The kinds of traits college admissions committees now call "lived experience."

The market no longer needs us to be useful—it needs us to be relatable.

It used to be the poor who lived those traits.

They knew hardship.

They sent sons to war, daughters to build new households.

They worked the land. They sacrificed.

They lived in tight-knit homes and let reality humble them daily. Not the daily grind—daily grit.

But now?

Everyone sort of survives. And wars are fought with drones.

Peter Sloterdijk describes it well: "We've moved from the realm of necessity to the space of pampering."

Struggle is no longer noble. It's not needed.

And yet—we crave it.

After centuries of trying to escape struggle, we now romanticize it.

My husband calls our kids "victims of abundance."

What he really means is: they lack struggle. They're unshaped by it.

I push back. "The environment doesn't demand it. They're adapted to the world we gave them."

But if we can't accept that everyone's equally human—and if we can't find enough relatable people who've been through real struggle—how will we decide who gets rewarded for it?

Maybe it'll all go performative.

The other day I watched Cory Booker break a Senate record—25 hours on the floor. He fasted beforehand so he wouldn't need a bathroom break.

Nancy Pelosi did a similar stretch—in heels. That kind of performative struggle.

Maybe we'll borrow it from earlier generations. Sheryl Sandberg recently posted about her great-great-grandmother fleeing Lithuania to escape religious persecution. It wasn't just a story or a point—it was a signal. A way to say: *I come from sacrifice.*

We want to be relatable. But the richer we get, the harder that gets.

I've left some of my struggle in the Postscript chapter—for my grandkids.

In case they ever need to borrow a little hardship to make the story land.

You're welcome, kiddos. Grandma loves you. (Use it wisely.)

Like in the Proximity Economy—where work became a signal, not a substance—maybe humanity will too.

So maybe it's the kids who run marathons.

Who take gap years teaching English in Guatemala.

Whose great-grandparents fought in Vietnam.

Kids who are multilingual.

Who play violin and soccer.

Who go to summer camps with ropes courses and leadership retreats.

Mock diplomacy summits.

"Emotional intelligence" workshops.

They won't face lived hardship. But they'll simulate it. Or borrow it.

Simulated negotiations. Controlled crises.

Deep research into ancestral pain.

Learn how to get yourself into trouble—and then out of it.

Maybe that's what "being human" will mean next.

Not surviving hardship, but performing the memory of it.

The poor won't be able to do that.

They've been pacified by screens. Flattened by sugar. Numbed by algorithms.

Maybe they have stories worth telling—but no network to perform them in.

They might still feel boredom.

But boredom doesn't count.

It doesn't boost your human score.

There has to be curated struggle.

Narrative-building afterward.

And a paper.

And a stamp.

So who will be giving this stamp?

And how do I make sure my kids get one?

I want to make sure they're among the ones allowed to signal their humanity—

So they can be stamped as real, raw, original humans—

So they can land the jobs close to the inherited machinery,

Where they'll act like they're innovating.

And receive the rewards they deserve.

My family is ready to compete for the stamp that says we're more human than the rest of you.

My kids will beat your kids.

THE LAST FREE CHILDREN

Rich parents are being called fascists by their own kids—for banning phones until age fourteen, handing them books, and expecting them to read. They enroll them in sports, make them play on teams where they learn to read social cues, cooperate, compete, and resolve conflict face-to-face. They send them to camps without WiFi, force them through boredom, through discomfort. They make them do hard things—hike uphill, sit through long dinners, endure silences. They teach them patience, frustration, how to navigate awkwardness without a screen to retreat into.

I am not a fascist parent. I am laissez-faire, with regret. On weekends, I pry the phones from their hands. On workdays, I let them govern themselves—a freedom they burn through too fast.

But I do what the rich do.

We send them to camps without phones, surrounded by trees. On weekends, I try to get them to cook one dish. The younger one trains in taekwondo and plays the cello. The older one ice skates. They walk to school. They have chores. The younger one helped her grandpa build a deck; the older one helped me put up wallpaper.

Like other rich parents, I see the loss of real human experience for kids. Too immersed in technology. Too sheltered by our worries—or maybe just neglected by our own distractions. So we engineer their environment—structuring discomfort, designing challenge, simulating struggle. It's not organic, like the rough, unsupervised world of the rural Balkans where my extended family lives.

There, discomfort happens naturally. Social cues, physical interaction, boredom, real struggle—it's just life. Authentic humanity.

We all opted out of that—for a reason.

I don't want to live like the Amish either.

But the rich have the option to buy back some of that discomfort.

Hardship—not as necessity, but as lifestyle.

Curated struggle.

Simulated grit.

But not all kids get to experience this.

I know a thirteen-year-old girl from Kupusina, a small village in Vojvodina, Serbia. I never call her—she calls me every day. Afternoon her time, morning mine. We FaceTime—fifteen minutes, on average—just to check in.

Unlike my extended family who still live in the remote mountains in Bosnia—mostly disconnected from the virtual world, she is fully plugged in—endless digital access, but a scarcity of real, physical experiences.

Her mother—my first cousin—is no longer there. She lives with her grandmother in what was once a farm. The animals are gone.

The village is still rich in natural resources—fertile land, dense woods along the Danube, an abundance of fish.

But people don't depend on those anymore.

The town is virtually connected, but economically left behind. Abandoned houses line the streets.

Some farmers still work large plots of land, and a nearby beer factory helps sustain the local economy. But many have moved to Germany for work. Her grandmother tells me they bathe and care for the elderly there.

The girl spends nearly every waking hour on a device—I can see it in her "last active" status.

She doesn't read books. There's no library in her town.

Every time we FaceTime, she's drinking an energy drink, eating candy or chips. When her friend comes over, they drink something called Kleiner Klopfer—a German liquor with a cartoonish design, rainbow border, and a grinning mascot that mimics the look of children's candy. Brightly packaged, it contains 16.4% alcohol—about as strong as fortified wine. It's marketed as the world's loudest party drink, but it looks like it was plucked straight from a toy aisle. It's not just irresponsible—it's devious. Predatory. A calculated strategy to blur the line between childhood and adult intoxication. And it works.

It's daylight outside, but you wouldn't know—her room is dark, curtains drawn, lit only by the purple glow of the LED lights. She thinks they're cool. For her birthday, I asked what she wanted. Roblox credit. She wanted to dress her avatar. I sent real clothes instead. The size was too big. She has to wait another year to wear them.

I texted her father, who lives in another country, begging him to tell his mother—her grandmother—to stop buying her Klopfer, energy drinks and candy. She's drinking too many. She's pale. She rarely goes outside.

When I pleaded with her to find a book, any book, she told me she was reading Girl in Pieces.

I looked it up—a novel that romanticizes self-harm and trauma. Cultural garbage, exported by America to the world.

I asked her not to read it. Told her I was writing a book and maybe she'd help design the cover. She jolted from her world, eager—sketching, brainstorming, alive with ideas. She's just thirteen, but the instinct for meaningful work is already there.

Her English is almost as good as her ethnic Hungarian, and she speaks no Serbian—despite living in Serbia.

One time she called from a bar. I was furious and demanded she hand the phone to a waiter who had just served her another energy drink.

"Lady, it's not against the law," he said.

"But she's thirteen. How can she even be in a bar?"

"It's not against the law."

Later, I realized—the bar is the only enclosed space they have to hang out in winter. And it's better than home where she would be on her device. At least there, she's with friends. At least she feels less alone.

I felt stupid for making a scene.

She's left the village only a few times. Everything she knows about life comes through a screen. Some nights, she has *phone sleepovers* with a friend who lives far away—leaving the phone on the pillow, video glowing next to her face, as they fall asleep.

For weeks, she was a therian—someone who believes they are spiritually connected to, or even are, a non-human animal. She spent hours practicing how to jump on all fours. Now, she's saving up for a therian mask—a gray cat, handcrafted on Etsy, $89 plus shipping.

She doesn't just want to be a therian. She wants to own the costume. The internet sold her an identity—with accessories.

Now she idolizes Melanie Martinez, listens to songs that turn trauma into an aesthetic, dysfunction into an identity. She is saving money to buy Melanie's merch—plastic bags and a Crybaby necklace.

She called me one afternoon while my kids were out on the lake, their kayaks gliding in sync. She was indoors, past midnight—curtains drawn, bathed in purple light, scrolling, alone.

The internet feeds her algorithmic trash. She belongs to BigTech's world.

But not entirely.

Her grandmother is sewing her a traditional Hungarian dress for her cousin's wedding—blue flowers, delicate lace. She showed it to me on video. It's beautiful.

We talk about America often. She wouldn't want to live here—but she wants to try McDonald's, KFC, Starbucks. She knows the menus, but she's never tried any of it.

Sometimes she tells me about her day while upside down, doing a handstand against the wall. Her cartwheels aren't great—but she thinks they're amazing.

The glow of the screen is still there. But still—something breaks through. A spark that hasn't been flattened yet.

It's not the poverty. Not really. There's scarcity, yes—but there's also enough.

She showed me her bathroom. The tub was so old and rusted it had more black than white. She told me they have an outdoor bathroom too that she sometimes uses. Not really a bathroom—just a potty hole, built with old boards.

Basic amenities are lacking. But what's scarier isn't the rusted tub. It's the *other* kind of excess.

The overconsumption of information.

The overindulgence in noise.

I think back to my childhood. I was often bored.

What would I have done with device in my hands?

The World Wide Web in my hands.

And yet—it's not worldly.

Not wide.

Not a web.

It's isolating.

Flattening.

A bubble.

The children of the wealthy—banned from screens, forced into real-world experiences—might be the last free children.

Free range. Pasture raised.

There's a quote: "The future is already here—it's just not evenly distributed."

Not just unevenly distributed. Unevenly selected.

The rich know what to embrace and what to avoid.

There's a pile of future to consume.

But those with means are skipping the junk, dodging the traps, curating their children's reality while they still can.

How much longer can they keep it up?

Why do we stand by as it slips away from everyone else's kids?

FULL, MESSY, UNPREDICTABLE PEOPLE

Those with the means will define what it means to be human. But what it means isn't what it is—or what it was. And sometimes I feel we're all losing the real thing.

When I go to the Balkans—especially to the rural mountain areas where some of my family lives—I see more organic humanity. And I'm not just talking about less mobile signal, less technology, more reliance on physical tools, on the land, on each other.

It's in how they carry themselves. Their faces are more animated—like they still use the full range of facial muscles that haven't atrophied. They don't filter as much. They still blush. Even grandmas blush.

They say what they need. They anticipate what I might need. Sometimes wrongly—packing me a small meal before I leave, just in case. Because you never know. The land is harsh.

Even their aesthetics are different—the way they age, the way they arrange their lives and spaces. It's minimalism, but the real kind. They pack more meaning into it. They still have pride. They still have honor. That's passé here. Our aesthetics are getting weird. The latest trend is the "aliengelic" look—makeup that makes skin appear poreless. Like glass. Like a machine.

Too many people have lost faith in anything transcendental. Too much ambient influence—vibes, aesthetics, energy—has worn us down in ways we don't fully see.

I like meeting new people, but I can't shake the sense that most relationships are transactional. It's not paranoia—I can just feel it. And it's such a turnoff. You'd think abundance would eliminate the need for transactional ties. There's no famine—yet it still circulates. My husband says I'm in my own bubble. That I'm imagining it. That I read too much into things.

But even the relationship with him gets weird. He sends me polished, AI-generated text messages in the middle of an argument—either to prove a point or to apologize. He screenshots my message, feeds it into the AI with a prompt like, *"Reply to this so she's not mad,"* and sends me back the response.

He thought I wouldn't notice.

The tone was right. But the grammar and punctuation were too right.

He's against offshoring tech jobs—but he offshored the argument with his wife to AI.

And yes, maybe in some rawer version of the Balkans, the fight wouldn't even exist—because my sensitivities, my expectations, might be artificial.

Politicians sound like robots—scripted, hollow. My managers and coworkers did too, especially when they spoke to clients. Their words felt preloaded; their responses rehearsed. Press-release language.

Even when I meet with friends, the first hour is just us rehashing our feeds. They don't notice, and I don't say anything—but it feels like I'm scrolling them. News, memes, outrage-of-the-day. Whatever the algorithm served up gets passed around like conversation. Usually, it's some hypocrisy in the world. That's what sells. I try to steer things deeper, but it never lands. Or maybe it's just that my friends are men.

People have been optimized. Smoothed out. Pride became self-branding. Emotional intelligence became presentation management. Virtue got reduced to signaling.

Even the way we move is different. Everyone feels restrained. The edges dulled. Fewer uncalculated gestures. Fewer grand expressions. More moderation. Call it civilized if you want. It still feels like a loss.

I think I'm surrounded by people who are less human. Not as in virtue but in demeanor. But maybe that's just a start, maybe it eventually affects virtue. Or maybe we still have that raw humanity, but it never gets to be practiced—because our environment no longer calls for it.

They say we're running on "old hardware." That we're wired to eat when food is in front of us, to store calories for famine. But in a world of abundance, that wiring is bad. Old hardware. Even our metaphors betray us.

And then, the kids. They should be the most human—young and unfiltered. But their instincts get channeled into inhuman things. I hide the iPads; they find them. Then they hide them from me. I call their names, get distracted by my own device—until I finally find them, hunched in a dark closet, faces bathed in blue light.

The time they could have spent creating something real, resolving conflicts with their sister, or cleaning their room—gone. Replaced by scrolling through hair tutorials or watching a TikTok of someone squeezing a pimple.

I once got so mad I slammed the phone to the floor—pieces of the screen flew everywhere. A week later, I was at the repair shop. Some nights I was ready to take them to the lake at dawn and toss the devices in. A purge. A reset. By morning, I was making coffee, already thinking about other things.

I came across a study recently titled "Have Humans Passed Peak Brain Power?" It found that over a third of adults in the U.S. can no longer evaluate basic logical statements or apply simple mathematical reasoning. The percentage is rising across all high-income countries. Some blame phones. Others point to genetics, air pollution, long COVID—maybe even regular use of ChatGPT.

It's not what I imagined when they were born. I imagined they'd surpass me. I still want them to. But it's not even about that.

If they never reach the full potential of their cognitive sovereignty—something fundamental is lost.

The full experience of being human means pushing up against the ceiling of what their brains, their biology, their nature makes possible.

And in an age of abundance, they should be able to reach it.

But somehow, what we've created—the life of distraction—might rob them of that.

I don't like thinking like this. Maybe I'm wrong. Maybe they'll surprise me. I hope they do.

But if they grow up and find jobs in Proximity Economy where they will signal innovation at work like I did—that'll seal the deal. Because there's nothing more dumbing down, more numbing down, than that. As kids, they numb their brains with devices because they want to. As adults, when they learn to control the devices, they'll enter the Proximity Economy—where the system will finish the job.

The system needs people to justify itself—but it wants to run them like software. It pretends to want more humanity. Universities and corporations now talk about "human skills," as if empathy and intuition are the future. But what they really need is less humanity.

The Proximity Economy rewards smoothness, predictability—signalers, followers, suck-ups. It doesn't want real people. It wants workers who are barely human at all.

Sometimes I feel like someone's messing with me. All these contradictions—I don't know how to explain them.

And that's what makes it hard to prepare them for the future. I just want to give them a shot at becoming full, messy, unpredictable people. But it's hard. I'm up against two forces: an external world designed to automate them, and their own instinct reaching for the machine. And some days, I don't know which side is winning.

But I know the stakes.

And surrender isn't an option.

HARD RESET

MARCHING UNDER BOMBS

Before work became signaling, before motherhood, before performance reviews, before America—I had a front-row seat to something else.

At twenty, I had already been married for two years. My husband, twenty-three, and I wore targets—bright red bullseyes—like the Target store logo—pinned to our shirts. We carried banners. We chanted. We protested. We dared.

It was the spring of 1999, and NATO was bombing Serbia. Jets roared above, striking infrastructure below. But we—the youth—marched through the streets, fearless, maybe a little crazy.

By day, we hitchhiked from the refugee center in the mountains to Novi Sad—the nearest big city—to protest. I imagine an American pilot looking down at us through his scope, watching us flip him off. Smiling. Knowing we'd end up in America—because that's how these stories are supposed to go.

By night, we hitchhiked back to the mountain, climbed to our lookout point, and watched the city burn.

Just months earlier, it had been our makeout spot. A front-row seat to the city lights, to hope, to the future we imagined. Then came the bombing. Our spot—where we kissed, where we dreamed—became a front-row seat to destruction.

When the oil refinery was hit, the night sky turned to hellfire. It was biblical.

We watched as the last of the three bridges across the Danube was attacked day after day, but somehow it held. It stood against all odds. Like it stood for something.

But then, one night in late April, more missiles came. They hit their target—and the bridge finally collapsed.

Unlike the refinery, it wasn't spectacle. It was sadness.

It wasn't just a bridge. It was a connection.

We called it the rail bridge—a massive steel structure with a lane for pedestrians, a lane for cars, and a lane for trains. The one we used to cross to get to school.

And we knew we couldn't protest anymore. We were stranded on the wrong side of the river. The Serbian army built a makeshift pontoon ferry to cross the Danube, but by then, the excitement—the novelty of bombing and protests in the main square—had worn off. The mood of resistance had shifted to survival, then acceptance, then normalization. The unthinkable became routine.

But at least we fought.

THE SILENCE
OF THE STREETS

've marched alongside Americans a few times. Immigration rallies at St. Louis Airport when Build the Wall was at its peak, MeToo in St. Louis, then for BLM. But I've never felt as moved, as determined, as I did in Novi Sad, Serbia during 1999, flipping off American pilots in NATO jets overhead.

Maybe the pilot was French.

But the bombs? We knew whose they were. Definitely American. My kids are American. I am too. Maybe because of them, I try. But part of me still can't forgive this country.

Still, because of my kids, I participate in protests here. They deserve a better system. I deserve a better system.

But let's be honest—American protests are often about symbolism: race, gender, echoes of the past. Symbols get people into the streets far more than economic injustice ever does. Even when economic protests do spark, they rarely last. Occupy Wall Street fizzled—maybe because it lacked a clear enemy. Identity-based protests have one.

Economic suffering doesn't.

So who do you blame for the Proximity Economy?

Well, here's a starter list—in case someone wants to take it to the streets:

— The laptop class.

— Corporate executives.

— Big corporate headquarters, with their fountains and neatly mown lawns.

— Government bureaucrats.

— Visa and Mastercard—skimming value from every transaction on earth.

— Banks—capital's gatekeepers, siphoning fees from the rest of us.

— Wall Street.

— Accenture and McKinsey, selling PowerPoint strategy to aging empires.

— Global IT outsourcers that help aging empires create noise and signal innovation.

— Lobbyists.

— Jeff Bezos

— Marc Andreessen, author of the techno-optimist manifesto

— Economists who still pretend the Proximity Economy doesn't exist.

— The believers in meritocracy, who think proximity to algorithms is deserved and rational.

I like what Elon Musk is doing with DOGE—so of course he's not on the list. I'd like him even more if someone whispered DOCE in his ear and he woke up the next day building that instead—same energy.

But even knowing who's to blame doesn't mean people act. Maybe it's comfort. Or maybe this country is just too big—too vast, too fractured to move as one. Maybe it's this prevailing belief that the system works. Institutions function. Unemployment is low. There are always jobs, so whatever economic suffering comes your way, it's on you.

When we lived in Portland, Oregon, I walked to work from 11th to 1st Avenue, passing through the downtown park blocks, occasionally touching trees, weaving between scores of homeless people sprawled on benches, on the grass, filling the park. I had never seen so many in one place. The instinct is to help. But there are too many. You watch how others navigate—stepping around, looking past—and you learn to do the same.

They noticed me. Some smoked, and if I was pushing my kids in the stroller, they'd turn their heads, exhaling in the other direction— small gestures of consideration.

I noticed them. Some sat on benches, just waking up, drinking something warm. Their blankets were neatly folded—army style. You could tell they had lived a different kind of life. That they still cared.

In the Balkans, family ties run deeper. We keep them home— sometimes out of love, sometimes out of shame. But at the very least, we feed them. They have shelter.

And when there's injustice—real or perceived—something that really cuts deep, people move. They take to the streets.

Sixteen people recently died in Novi Sad when railway station canopy collapsed. The protests have been nonstop—students, workers, people marching for weeks, months.

It's the residue of communism, I think—that instinct for collective responsibility. They don't live in a better system. The U.S. is far better organized, with more stable structures, more credible institutions. But the muscle of revolt is stronger there. It lifts more people. It lasts longer before fizzling out.

In 2013, there was a small protest in front of the Lincoln Memorial. I was there. A group of Bosnians stood holding signs, sending a message of solidarity with protests back home. Even from America, we fought. In Bosnia, an infant had died—she couldn't cross state lines for medical treatment because government inaction had left newborns without personal ID numbers. The parents, desperate, took it to the streets. Crowds gathered outside Sarajevo's parliament, demanding immediate action.

The movement gained momentum, cutting across ethnic lines—Bosniaks, Croats, and Serbs, all united. We lived in D.C. then, and we marched too. Bosnian news covered it—Bosnians protesting in front of the Lincoln Memorial.

The government caved. The law passed.

The bureaucratic lapse was fixed.

Results—immediate.

Yesterday, CNN reported that two kids—ages two and nine—froze to death in Detroit. Their mother had been calling shelters, leaving messages that were never returned. For months, they lived in a van. A few nights ago, she parked in a casino garage, hoping it would be enough. It wasn't. They froze to death.

Nothing. No mass protests. No outrage. Not even a local outcry.

Why did this mother not have a home?

For every mother without a home, there's another—one like me—working a fake job in the Proximity Economy, earning a paycheck that exists to justify inefficiencies, not create anything real. I'm part of the system that failed her. So is my husband—trapped in abstractions. So is my friend, the Washington Insider, juggling four credential-heavy, irrelevant roles that produce nothing. And so are thousands of others.

Mass protests don't always lead to systemic change. But here, they don't even happen.

And when nothing happens—on the streets or in the halls of power—when the federal government self-perpetuates, when thousands of bullshit jobs get created in DC, when weird programs get funded with taxpayer money—something else forces it to stop.

Systemic collapse doesn't arrive with a warning. It creeps in while everyone assumes things will keep working. Bureaucracies expand. Departments exist just to justify themselves. Inefficiencies pile up. Wealth pools at the top under the guise of expertise. The Proximity Economy thrives, funneling resources to those closest to power—coddling them like newborns—while real babies freeze in a van.

Complacency isn't just for elites. It belongs to anyone comfortable enough to look away. And that's when something else—something like DOGE—steps in. A hard reset, triggered when the public is too passive or the system too entrenched to correct itself.

DOGE doesn't negotiate; it executes. It has the power to shut down buildings, access Treasury systems, and fire entire agencies. It grew in the vacuum left by inaction—bloated with waste, inefficiency, and fraud.

Americans won't dismantle the Proximity Economy.

DOGE is dismantling the establishment in DC. From what I have seen, they are targeting the right agencies: USAID, ED, CDC.

DOCE will do the same to markets. No one voted for it. No one debated it. But it will come.

Would it be better—more inspiring—if change came from the people? If they took to the streets, demanded, forced, won? Of course. History would look better on film 100 years from now. It would give some future director material for the next great political epic. The next *Selma*, the next *Battleship Potemkin*.

But that's not how this ends.

More likely, someone—maybe a pragmatic populist, another Bernie, or even Trump—will step in and do what neither the system nor the people would. And when that happens, I won't be standing in the way.

My husband and I didn't vote in the 2024 election. He supports Trump but says wars feel inevitable, no matter who's in office. He stopped voting after Obama "screwed Libya from behind," as he puts it—his way of describing the U.S. strategy to "lead from behind" during the NATO intervention in Libya, after which the country descended into long-term instability.

"I don't want blood on my hands," he says.

I planned to vote for Trump but didn't take advantage of early voting. Then Election Day came, and I was unexpectedly in Pittsburgh for business.

Coincidentally, both Trump and Harris were in town that day—holding rallies in different parts of the city.

That night, I had dinner with my coworkers. Someone asked who I was hoping would win.

"I hope Trump wins," I said.

They were relieved to be talking to someone on the same team.

Some of them told me they'd already voted for Trump. Others, on H-1B visas, couldn't vote—but they supported him.

All Indian men. "He'll be better for business," they said.

I didn't want him to be good for *our* kind of business.

I want him to tear it all apart—this trip, this dinner, this conversation, this whole setup.

My voting history has been all over the map—Sanders in the 2016 primaries, Clinton in the general, an independent in 2020, and supporting but not voting for Trump in 2024.

I saw Trump as a wrecking ball—someone who might expose inefficiencies and 'bullshit jobs' in Washington, D.C., with the hope that the disruption would ripple into the Proximity Economy and its rent-seeking corporations. I'm still keeping my fingers crossed.

THEY WEREN'T
MEANT TO BE DIVIDED

St. Louis is politically diverse. When we lived in the Shaw neighborhood, I used to run along Flora Avenue—tree-lined, landscaped, one of the city's most beautiful. Every October, the Shaw Art Fair takes place there. It's a wide avenue but quiet, with slow, low traffic.

At the height of the BLM protests, I started counting American flags and BLM signs on people's lawns.

I walk. I touch some trees. I count.

The houses had either one or the other. Never both. It was a political identity mapped onto front lawns.

I don't remember the exact count, but I remember that the American flags won—just by a few.

Most people in Shaw probably know people from both camps. I do. In fact, as opposite as it gets—polar extremes.

My next-door neighbor was a tall guy, athletic build, a beard, a classic manly man. Republican. He was a few years older than me, with a son and daughter just a few years older than my girls, who were three and four at the time. He and his wife had an amicable divorce. He'd visit the kids, sometimes stay over at his ex-wife's house, and I'd hear them talking, laughing on the patio.

I'd step outside and joke, "Are you two sure you're divorced?"

"Oh yeah," they'd assure me.

He'd toss a ball with his kids on the street. For Halloween, he went all in—fire pit going, hot dogs sizzling, handing them out to neighborhood kids as they trick-or-treated.

Our street was a cul-de-sac, closed off from South Grand Ave, where traffic hummed and life could be violent and messy—not just in crime reports, but in the sirens and gunshots we heard. We didn't own guns, but the Manly Man did.

During the BLM protests, when riots spilled onto South Grand and stores were getting smashed, the mom across the street and I came up with a plan. If things got out of control—if windows started breaking—we'd grab the kids and head straight to the Manly Man's house, leaving our husbands behind.

Our husbands debated the news. He would stand in the street.

Even outside of the protests, our cul-de-sac had its moments. A few times, cars sped into the dead end. The second he heard them, he'd storm out of his house, plant himself in the middle of the street, and wait. As the driver turned, trying to slip away guilt-free, the manly man would block his path—arm outstretched, standing his ground, unmoving as the car approached.

The car would stop.

He'd slam his hands on the hood, circle around, and lean into the window.

"There's a sign, you idiot! There are kids on this street."

The rest of the neighborhood watched from porches and windows, silent but approving. The sheer audacity of it—standing in front of a moving car, refusing to flinch. It was admirable.

Our kids went to the same woke school, where teachers were required—and parents were strongly encouraged—to take Anti-Bias, Anti-Racist (ABAR) training. There was a teacher there with painted nails, long dyed blond hair, and some makeup.

He didn't like him.

"I don't think he should be working in that school," he told me.

I mentioned that once, while waiting in the school lobby, I saw him at the whiteboard, explaining compound interest to a few seventh graders.

"He was all in, held their attention, did a great job," I said.

He still didn't like him.

He was a commercial refrigeration guy, fixing walk-in coolers and ice machines for businesses. He dabbled in HVAC work on the side. Sometimes, when the school needed a repair, he'd volunteer to take a look before they had to pay someone.

He bounced between jobs—sometimes working for a small refrigeration company, sometimes trying to make his own business work. He was great at his trade but not at running a business.

Over time, his work started drying up. The economy was shifting in ways that didn't favor independent tradesmen. And then COVID happened.

He was working, but it weighed on him—he wanted to keep everyone else healthy, especially since his ex-wife and their kids were living with her parents at the time, between homes. His time with the kids became less and less. They never returned to an even split.

Life kept moving, though, in its uneven way. The neighborhood settled back into its usual rhythm, people carried on.

One warm, sunny day a friend of mine came to visit. She's from Bosnia, like me. But she suffered more loss in the war, including a parent who was killed by the ethnic group my husband and I are associated with.

It's something we rarely talk about, but when we do, it lingers. Apologizing is strange. But silence is stranger.

She's the Earth Mother type—kumbaya incarnate. Tattoos, loose, flowy clothes, artsy, deeply spiritual, into body-and-soul healing. She fosters animals, does yoga, wishes she could afford a therapist—and thinks those of us who can are crazy for not having one. She doesn't like Trump—Elon Musk, even less.

She is an ally to all—Black people, immigrants, LGBTQ+, Native Americans, women, Mother Nature. She hates capitalism, distrusts the police, and speaks out against brutality. If there's a protest in St. Louis for a marginalized group, she's there.

She has one child in a private school with a philosophy that rejects mainstream education—hands-on, nature-focused, free from screens and standardized testing. A place they can barely afford.

She would go hungry before pulling her kid out of that school.

She doesn't just critique the patriarchy—she moves through its weight, feeling it in every institution. Education, policing, finance, even parenting norms. She's not performatively woke; she embodies her ideology, down to barefoot shoes and a refusal to engage in structured work.

As Earth Mother was leaving my house, she saw the Manly Man outside. They started talking while I watched from the window, frozen—two planets colliding.

I tried to read lips, trace body language, waiting for something—anything—to shift. But it was just murmurs. A few minutes passed. Then she got in her car and left.

At the time, I thought it was nothing. But it stayed with me.

In some parallel universe, that moment plays out differently.

They stand there, still speaking in low voices, the air heavy, thick. I am at the window, watching. Then, suddenly, as if pulled by some unseen force, they both turn.

Their heads move in eerie unison. Their eyes lock onto mine.

The line is redrawn. It's not between the two of them anymore.

It's between me, hidden behind the glass, and them.

I shrink back.

They saw me.

They know how I make my money.

They look back at each other. Disappointed.

And as it settles—while she drives home—it grows.

Not just disappointed. Pissed.

They realized they had more in common with each other than either of them did with me.

Their houses were under $200K; I owned a few. One had an American flag, the other a BLM sign. I had neither.

He was underemployed, she was unemployed, and I was overemployed.

Not because of merit, or effort, but because of how the economy is wired.

But their struggles mirrored each other more than either mirrored mine.

They worried about the tangible, the immediate. Earth Mother's son had several surgeries after an accident—bills piling up, the slow grind of recovery. He wrestled with depression, the instability of his work, and property taxes that kept climbing as the neighborhood's value outpaced his income.

I worried too, but at a different altitude.

Not about food, rent, or medical debt.

Not about immediate family, not about myself.

My worries stretched across borders, across time zones—extended family, currency fluctuations, tragic stories of people I once knew but wasn't close to, contract renewals, missed appointments, kids glued to their phones.

They taped their windows and disconnected radiators to save on heating bills. I carved out a month in Vail, sipping mulled wine under patio heaters.

They spent their summers in St. Louis; I spent mine in Europe.

I built presentations so an executive could nod and say 'cool,' while he was in some attic fixing the actual cooling system for an entire school.

She tried to join the system, but it never had a place for her.

He fought to stay afloat, but scarcity kept pulling him under.

I picture them both in a Mastercard conference room. Laptops open. Corporate theater unfolding.

The Manly Man wouldn't last a day.

He'd stand up and leave—no explanation, no hesitation.

The Earth Mother might try. She'd want to blend in, play along just long enough to keep affording the private school.

But her nature would betray her.

Eventually, she'd say something too blunt, refuse to parrot the script, roll her eyes at the wrong moment.

She wouldn't just quit.

She'd rage quit. Like last time.

That was then.

Where are they now?

He's gone.

He killed himself two years ago.

He was loved. He was needed.

He just couldn't feel it. Couldn't see it.

She's grown more radical.

Maybe not out of defeat—but out of clarity.

THE ZOO ANIMAL ARGUMENT

Most of the people I worked with had side gigs on top of their full-time jobs—whatever full-time even means. Nobody really works eight hours.

First, it's simply not possible to signal for that long.

Second, the dream of working less—popularized by books like *The 4-Hour Workweek*—has become mainstream.

Third, since ChatGPT arrived, generating noise at work—projecting productivity—has never been easier.

The moment someone gets laid off, they slap the green *Open to Work* banner on LinkedIn—then update their profile with a new job. A side gig suddenly becomes a full-time role. A new consulting venture appears overnight.

One of my former coworkers runs a Hotworx franchise. Another teaches cycling three times a week. A third designs websites with his daughter. A fourth trades commodities. I manage short-term rentals.

But nobody is a zoo animal. That's what Marc Andreessen wrote in his techno-optimist manifesto:

> We believe a Universal Basic Income would turn people into zoo animals to be farmed by the state. Man was not

meant to be farmed; man was meant to be useful, to be productive, to be proud.

"Farmed by the state"

Some boys watch too many horror movies and end up afraid of clowns.

Marc read too much Orwell and got scared of Big Bad UBI.

And did he even notice the contradiction? If people are meant to be useful and productive, how exactly would UBI turn them into zoo animals?

If we're wired to build, to contribute, to leave a mark—why would UBI change that?

We had side gigs while working. We kept them after we left.

Governments have been running UBI pilots for years, trying to determine if it works. But the real test already happened—salaries in the Proximity Economy are UBI.

People in the Proximity Economy get paid to make noise. That's the job.

My husband didn't get it. I told him I'd give up five-sixths of my salary just to stop signaling.

"And where would the remaining one-sixth come from?" he asked.

"From UBI," I said. "And five others would get a share of what's left—what hasn't been siphoned off to prop up one fake salary."

"But then... who would work your job?"

"Nobody would work my job!"

"Exactly," he said.

I stopped, watching him, waiting for the moment it would click. He was still confused.

"Who works now?" I asked.

"You do!"

"Doing what?"

Finally, the Aha moment.

So the question isn't whether UBI works—it already does.

Now, we just have to stop pretending it doesn't and formalize what's already happening. We're already pouring buckets of money on a few. Just spread it wider. Shower people with money.

"*Shower people with money.*" I wouldn't run an election campaign on that, but it would make a great T-shirt. If anyone's still looking for a side gig.

One person would be free from signaling. Five unemployed or underemployed people would get UBI.

And yet, nobody would sit still. Nobody *is* sitting still.

We start businesses. Trade commodities. Launch consulting firms. Manage short-term rentals.

Even celebrities aren't content just being rich. They create rosé brands and skincare lines—just to fill their time with tasks.

For many, the main gig is fake. The side gigs are real.

So no, Marc. We don't need capitalism to force us to be productive. We have already chosen to be. Even when the work is fake.

We create when we have time. We build when we're untethered. We're inspired when given space to think.

Where do we look more like zoo animals?

Out in the world, free to shape our own lives?

Or inside corporate walls, pacing in circles on anxiety meds, signaling for our next meal?

Marc Andreessen insists markets are "generative, not exploitative"— that a rising tide lifts all boats.

He is wrong.

A young PhD student at NYU modeled this. In his paper on Transformative AI, he wrote:

> When AI automates a job—whether a truck driver, lawyer, or researcher—the wages previously earned by the human worker don't vanish or automatically transform into broader economic gains. Instead, they flow to whoever controls the AI system performing that job.[23]

That's not generative. That's reallocation.

And it's not just AI. Even with older tech like the Switch—the benefits still flow to shareholders, executives and the managerial class, year after year, in perpetuity.

And sometimes, you don't even have to look *outside* corporate walls. The shift happens *within* them.

When Meta laid off thousands, their execs doubled their bonus potential to 200%. Not because of a breakthrough—just because their "independent compensation consultant" said it was justified. The average bonus paid to employees in Wall Street hit a record high for 2024, at $244,700, up 31.5% from the year before.[24]

The reallocation moved wealth upward.

But here's what I wonder. And I don't see people talk about this.

They talk about the race with China. Who's going to win the AI arms race?

---

23. [Caleb Maresca, "Strategic Wealth Accumulation Under Transformative AI Expectations," *arXiv preprint* arXiv:2502.11264v1 [econ.TH], February 16, 2025, New York University.]

24. "DiNapoli: Wall Street Bonus Pool Reaches Record High of $47.5 Billion in 2024." Office of the New York State Comptroller. March 28, 2025. https://www.osc.ny.gov/press/releases/2025/03/dinapoli-wall-street-bonus-pool-reaches-record-high-475-billion-2024

Everyone assumes we'll use AI to build—new things, new ideas.

But what if it's used to fortify instead?

What if corporations use AI to target vulnerabilities?

Dissent?

Let's say I publish this book on Amazon. And their AI flags it as a threat to the business. It critiques the Proximity Economy. It floats DOCE-style regulation—just enough to raise a flag. It doesn't say many nice things about Big Boss Jeff.

The AI reviews it. Scans for tone. Sentiment. Intent.

Not for quality. Not for truth. Just for threat.

It generates a flicker.

"Your book does not comply with our internal policies."

Orwell might still be relevant.

But maybe it's not the state we should fear—it's the network.

That's the new Big Bad Wolf.

THE INHERITED WORLD

SHE IS OURS

We live in Clayton, Missouri.

Washington University (WashU) is the centerpiece of the area—a stunning campus with Gothic architecture that evokes tradition, rigor, and permanence.

It generated a lot of news during the Gaza protests in the summer of 2024. The day after one protest, we went for a walk to observe the aftermath. Police were stationed all over campus, and as we passed one officer, we struck up a conversation. It turned out he was Bosnian, like us.

We shake hands and exchange names. He becomes the name, not the badge. Titles, uniforms, formality—it all dissolves. There is a shared language. The weight of unspoken history.

We asked him about the protests.

"Was yesterday the bad day?" I asked.

"Yes, it was. We had to cordon things off," he said. "Today we're just guarding the scheduled funeral on campus."

While we were talking, a woman in a black dress stepped up to him. "Thank you for everything you're doing," she said quietly. He nodded.

After she walked off, he shrugged. "She thanks me. But just a few minutes ago, a group of protesters walked by and told us to fuck off."

He didn't seem bitter. "I support them," he said. "The students. I support Palestinians too."

It made sense. Most Bosnian Muslims (Bosniaks) do. Bosnian Serbs, meanwhile, lean more toward Israel—not necessarily out of deep conviction, but because Bosniaks lean toward Palestine, and Serbs love nothing more than rooting for the opposite team. Our alignments are shaped more by history and emotion. It's rarely principle. Each side projects its own grievances onto distant struggles. But I suppose that isn't unique to Bosnians.

We chat some more and leave. As we walk back through the Clayton neighborhood, I wave to some school moms I know—some outside on their front porches, others jogging.

We walk along Wydown Boulevard and Alexander Drive, past some of the most beautiful houses. Not new—old glamour. Impeccable aesthetics.

There are no neighborhoods like this in Bosnia.

And yet, it's still hard to feel a sense of belonging in America.

The lifestyle is the same. I've assimilated.

It's the small things that feel different. Maybe they just add up.

If my kids forget their homework, I'll drive it to school, and the women say, "Let them fail and learn the hard way."

Their kids always say their please and thank yous, and they're polite enough—but they never ask, "How are you, Mrs. Majdov?" or "How was your day?" Sometimes they walk into my house without even saying hello. They don't look me in the eye. My kids aren't allowed to do that. Adults—especially seniors—have to be seen and acknowledged.

They travel with their husbands to "reconnect." I can imagine traveling—but traveling to reconnect? That's funny to me.

They follow shows; I prefer movies.

They keep things to themselves; maybe they think I don't.

Some have therapists; I call my mom.

Their ties to extended family seem loose.

I'm impatient. I often break rules. I am probably more judgmental.

They keep cats and dogs. We eat them.[25]

I think back to Bosnia, to a time when community wasn't something I had to seek out—it was just there. Once, as a child, I got into trouble with some neighborhood kids. A neighbor was about to set us straight when my grandfather walked by. He called me over and told the neighbor, "She's ours." That was it. The neighbor nodded, released me to my grandfather, and continued to scold the others.

Years later, I visited the remote mountain village where my mother grew up—a place with no roads to the houses, where every grave bore her maiden name. The whole village gathered in one house to see me. And I heard it again: "She's ours."

Simple. Grounding. A kind of belonging that needed no explanation. This was the community I was meant to inherit—passed down from my parents, my grandparents. I was supposed to tend to it, preserve it, and one day, pass it on to my daughters.

Yes, life would change. There would be modernity, cities, progress. But I wanted to keep the people.

There's no one here to say, "She is ours." Maybe it's gone everywhere. Maybe that's the real loss.

It's not just that the connection to land, to family, to the larger

---

25. A joke referencing a false claim Donald Trump made in 2024 about immigrants eating pets in Ohio.

web of relationships has been severed. Even cities feel hollowed out. Even nations. Even identities.

I don't think nationalism is inherently bad. It doesn't have to be aggressive—it can be communal, organic.

My first nation fractured. If Yugoslavia still existed, I most likely wouldn't be here.

If someone dared to build that kind of place again—not in name, but in spirit, in cohesion, in scale—a place where ethnicity remained visible and valued, but the real dividing lines were ideological: dynamism vs. stability, techno-optimism vs. humanism, globalism vs. nationalism—and the multiethnic fabric was preserved, not diluted, because it is cultural and beautiful—I wonder if we'd all come back.

Maybe my scattered family, across Chicago, Milwaukee, NYC, Austria, Germany, the Netherlands, would feel that same pull.

But no one dares imagine it.

A few years ago, while walking through WashU's campus, I noticed someone had glued a tiny Lenin figure to a pole—fist raised in defiance. A few days later, a group of young people handed me a pamphlet: *Fight for Socialism in Our Lifetime.* It was from the International Marxist Tendency, calling for a revolution inspired by Marx, Engels, Lenin, and Trotsky. I kept the pamphlet.

I remembered the refugee application forms I filled out in the late '90s to enter the U.S. One question stood out: *Have you or any member of your family ever belonged to the Communist Party?* I was too young during Yugoslavia's communist era to have been involved in anything myself. But finding someone from Yugoslavia without at least one relative in the Party is hard. I checked No.

And now, thirty years later, I'm handed an invitation—in Clayton, Missouri, of all places.

Youth is doing what youth has always done: experimenting, questioning, pushing boundaries. But economic uncertainty is making their voices louder. They see growing inequalities—of wealth, access, opportunity.

My daughters, for example, are more open to China. When TikTok was banned for a day, they immediately downloaded Xiaohongshu (Red Note), China's Instagram-like app. The algorithm dropped them into planet China—shiny new cities, bullet trains, stadiums, airports. Nothing cookie-cutter. Everything jaw-dropping.

"Can you take us there?" It was a glimpse of an alternative future.

Even Thomas Friedman agrees with them. He recently wrote an op-ed in NYT titled "I Just Saw the Future. It Was Not in America." He had visited Huawei's campus in China.

I've never been there. For all the travel I've done, I've never worked in China.

But I do wonder about that Huawei campus—monorail, labs, cafés, fitness centers.

What's under the hood? Not just what they'll produce—humanoids, AGI, triple-folding phones—but whether there will even be real demand for that future.

Maybe it's just me. I'm still on an iPhone 14.

Apple stopped innovating.

Maybe I'm just getting tired of the future.

First-generation immigrants are always some kind of mutant—caught between past and present, origin and destination. Too American for where we came from, never quite American enough for where we are.

But my daughters are Americans. The kind that look forward to the Super Bowl. They don't speak Chinese. They don't even speak Serbian. This is their home.

And if it were up to me, I wouldn't want America locked in some endless race with China.

I want America to build a future worth staying for—here.

They belong to this place, even if I never fully will.

THINGS THAT TAKE EFFORT

When COVID hit, I went fully remote. My husband had already been working from home before the pandemic.

Around the same time, I was trying to figure out if I could do something for my cousin's six-year-old son—the half-brother of the thirteen-year-old girl from Kupusina. He was living in an orphanage in Čitluk, Bosnia—an old-style one, run by nuns. In Bosnia, when things fall apart, family usually steps in. My cousin had two sisters who were in line to step in.

One had four small kids of her own and lived a life of scarcity in Bosnia. The other lived comfortably in the Netherlands. I made the call, just to see. The conversation didn't last long. I hung up, realizing she is definitely not the one. I felt the family's eyes turning to me. The next in line.

With schools shut down, we saw an opening. We started the process—adoption papers, lawyers. Packed up, flew to Bosnia.

We rented a house near Blagaj, a small town outside Mostar, so we could be close to the orphanage. It sat along a narrow street by the Buna River—so narrow we had to park the van in an open field and walk to the house. The street was lined with modest homes, grapevines, kiwis, and pomegranates. Patios draped with freshly washed laundry. Pots of flowers everywhere—a neighborhood where people have little but care deeply about beauty.

Some houses were pristine but unoccupied, their owners working in Western Europe, visiting once a year to deep clean before leaving again. Most were lived in, but scarcity was everywhere. The average income was about six hundred euros a month.

I enrolled the kids in an international school where they spoke English. We logged into Zoom calls to keep our jobs. We got the boy out of the orphanage and into our home, fostering while we waited. They told us others had the right to apply too.

The neighbors called us Amerikanci—Americans. I protested. We were Bosnians. We were born here. If there hadn't been a war, we would still live here.

But they kept saying it.

And maybe they had a point. We drove a van. Wore flip-flops. Did yoga in the backyard. Followed some faraway news they didn't care about—Wall Street, Silicon Valley, Washington, D.C. We worked from home on our laptops. Filled our glasses with ice. Spoke English with the kids.

We stood out, even if we didn't want to.

But over time, we became part of the street. We got to know their lives. They got to know ours.

There was a plot of no-man's-land where the neighbors planted vegetables. They offered us a section—the part closest to the house we were staying in.

One night, a fire broke out. It wasn't close yet, but if the wind shifted, it could spread fast. People got nervous. We started organizing—planning how to defend the homes if it came too close.

There was no garbage collection, so we took turns driving the trash to the city.

We dried laundry outside. Neighbors borrowed flour, sugar, oil. They came to ask us to translate things from English.

We shared vitamins and supplements—mostly collagen, which they didn't know could help with joint pain. One woman mentioned she was exhausted, so I gave her a B12 shot. Methylcobalamin—the good kind, straight from Hollywood. A few days later, more women showed up.

I thought about how none of them had hormones. No Myers' cocktails, no glutathione infusions. If only they knew. If only they had the chance to try.

You don't have to go through life feeling exhausted. Not if you know what to ask for—and can afford it.

They picked radishes and potatoes from their gardens, carrying them in their shirts. They brought them to us, dirt still clinging to the roots, drops of dew shimmering in the morning light.

I thought about America. The grocery stores. Produce scrubbed clean, sprayed for freshness, stripped of effort.

One day, a stray dog was hit by a car on the main road. There is no service to call. My husband dug the hole. I put its stiff body in a bag, dragged it to the field, and we buried it among wildflowers, ant mounds, and rocks.

The Buna River flooded the gardens. The kids got into trouble. Got out of trouble.

Six months passed just like that.

The adoption didn't go through. Our application was rejected. We met the couple who took him in—people who had waited years for adoption, nearly giving up. They couldn't have kids. We had more money, but they had more to give. More patience. More sacrifice.

A village. Grandparents downstairs, them upstairs. A garden behind the house. Aunts, uncles, cousins. A church. A community. A God the boy already knew—one the nuns had given him. The assurance, the hand-holding, the hope. Something he would have struggled to hold onto with us.

We tell ourselves we'll stay in touch. And so far, we have. So have the nuns.

The boy stayed. But I carried Blagaj with me. I was needed there. Maybe more than here. I try to engineer community in America, to find where I'm needed, but it's hard. Nuns do it so easily.

Things lose their meaning when they come too easily. Radishes. Money. People.

To love—you have to work for it.

You have to serve.

DEEP MISSOURI

We own a house deep in the woods in the middle of Missouri—a rare spot where the night sky is still untouched by light pollution. It's where I'm writing this book. When we're not here, we rent it out on short-term rental platforms.

It's so remote, we get only Panera delivered. Or sushi—if we trusted gas stations.

When I go there, people ask, "Where are you from? I detect an accent." In the city, nobody asks. There's diversity. I'm just another person.

But here, they sometimes slow their sentences—like I just got off a boat.

I don't mind. I'm curious about them too.

It's a deeply forested area, dotted with farms, cows, horses, and tractors. The average lot size is six acres—we have only three, but others with farms have ten. There's plenty of land around each house, yet it's still one division—people know who belongs and who doesn't.

The birds here are striking—small, colorful ones flitting between the trees, larger circling overhead.

And sometimes, a family of white albino deer moves through, ghostlike against the dark woods.

My family loves coming here—there's always something to do. Plant tomatoes and flowers, trim bushes, extend the deck, feed the birds, build things for the kids. I teach them to drive. I'm not supposed to, but they're tall and can reach both pedals.

We wait until it's dark, when no one's out on the subdivision road and no one can see us. Then we get in the car—one at the steering wheel, me in the passenger seat, the other in the back.

We put on music and drive slow loops through the subdivision. Full moon above, the headlights catch the fireflies, then vanish as we pass.

Sometimes I imagine one of them, forty years from now, driving me to the hospital. I'm having a heart attack. Or some other final crisis. Last day on Earth. Moon overhead, like before.

I look over and say, *"Remember the fireflies? You were twelve. You were driving under a full moon."*

She rolls her eyes and says, *"Mom, not now."*

But she remembers.

I like to imagine the drama—the emotionally manipulative kind. If it were the final scene of a movie, I'd probably cringe.

The house is surrounded by tall trees. A dense wooded stretch all around. They stand quiet and still. The bark is dark, rough, and deeply grooved. The kind I like to touch most.

I sourced most of the furniture from Facebook Marketplace, one of the few features of Facebook I love and use. There's no greater thrill than finding original mid-century pieces on it. Why buy new from China when I can get '60s Yugoslavia?

Our neighbors in the woods are mostly families. Some are multi-generational, with two houses on the same land. There are also retired seniors. American flags and Trump flags stay up long after elections.

Some houses have roadside Jesus posters—those are permanent. Gunshots in the distance are a constant. The Second Amendment isn't just a slogan here; it's lived.

There's one Black teenager on our street. He's adopted or fostered. When we first moved in, his father introduced himself right away and told us about him. "He is ours." Familiar language. I noticed.

At first, I found it strange—why mention the boy's race at all? But then I understood. He was preempting any assumptions. Making sure we knew he belonged. Just in case.

Same words. But different stakes.

Then he invited my husband to come and practice shooting with him. He has a shooting range. Bring the kids, he said.

People don't fit neatly into categories.

We love the nature around the house and go for runs often. Neighbors walk their dogs and stop to talk—about the weather, local news, what's happening with other neighbors. And then come the bigger conversations. For some, the main enemy is still Russia—the Cold War version, the one they remember. The war in Ukraine registers, but Trump's shifting geopolitical strategy doesn't.

I don't know exactly what most of them do for income. Some are retired. Some run small businesses. Some just work the land. There's a local doctor with a greenhouse full of exotic plants. A veterinarian down the road. One oddball with a roadside Jesus poster obsession.

Even the professionals here seem to split their time—part clinic, part soil. They don't just work jobs; they tend to things. Few seem to depend on tech, government programs, or corporate payroll. Their survival feels closer to the ground.

But for all the talk of personal freedom and rugged individualism—the

First and Second Amendments—this place runs on rules. Self-imposed ones, which is fascinating in a place that prides itself on freedom.

If I drive a little too fast—40 in a 25—I get a message from the neighborhood watch. Someone was speeding.

Neighbors are watching.

When we bought the house, some neighbors were furious that we listed it on short term rental platform. They called meetings, pushed for a ban. I had read the bylaws before buying—there were no restrictions. But they voted anyway. No more short-term rentals. Their lawyer informed them of grandfather laws—if you owned before the rule, you got to keep renting. Some still don't like me for it. My daughter baked apple tarts for some of the older couples. It worked for a few weeks. Then I drove 40 in a 25 again, and it wore off.

There's an abandoned house deep in the woods. The girls love to explore it. A woman nearby hates this—calls me, threatens to call the sheriff. The house isn't hers. She doesn't even know the owners. But she tells the kids to leave. They ignore her. She threatens again. They say, Fine, call the sheriff.

They come home giddy from getting in trouble. Then they ask, "What if the sheriff actually comes?"

I tell them they'll have to talk to him. And while they explain, they should remind him: "You were a kid once too."

They love the plan. They hope the sheriff comes just so they can tell him.

Maybe in a place with fewer rules, people create their own, just to stay busy.

The sheriff might have bigger things to deal with. Then again, maybe not. Crime is low.

There is always work here.

Lawnmowers buzz, snow piles up, wind does damage, things break, things grow.

Still, the human impulse to over-engineer is everywhere. Some neighbors try to tame the woods, make it look like the suburbs. That annoys me. It's not just me who feels less free here. Sometimes even nature looks cornered.

My kids have been yelled at for stepping over invisible property lines. Guests, scolded for fishing in a shared lake.

My husband bought and put up signs, one on each side to warn our guests that our neighbors might yell at them if they cross beyond. A relic from another era:

YOU ARE LEAVING THE AMERICAN SECTOR.
ВЫ УХОДИТЕ ИЗ АМЕРИКАНСКОГО СЕКТОРА

A vintage Berlin Wall warning. Cold War history.

"They won't get it," I told him.

He shrugged. "Doesn't matter. We do."

THE STABILIST
PROPOSAL

THE WELL OF HOARDERS

We've been saying *afuera* in my house ever since Argentinian President Javier Milei's video. There's something deeply satisfying about watching him peel stickers off a whiteboard—each one labeled with a ministry he shut down—and say *afuera, afuera, afuera*. It means: out. Canceled. Gone.

Every sticker he peeled gave me a small, satisfying hit of endorphins.

Elon Musk tried to recreate the energy when they announced DOGE with a chainsaw. It didn't hit the same.

Yesterday, I read an article in *The Economist* titled: "Inheriting is becoming nearly as important as working." The argument? Younger generations are locked out—unless they inherit. The author called it *inheritocracy*.

It's not just the ultra-rich. The typical heir isn't getting a superyacht—they're inheriting a house, or the proceeds from its sale. And the financial industry knows it. Wealth management services are multiplying, eager to capture the flood of legacy money.

I see headlines like: "The Shockingly Easy Ways to Build Generational Wealth." Or: "Want to Set Your Kids Up for Retirement? So-and-so, aka 'Mrs. Dow Jones,' Shares the Three Accounts That Could Help."

The Economist concluded, "This is dangerous for capitalism and society."

Although, at some point, we have to ask: is this even capitalism?

If two-thirds of the economy is the Proximity Economy, if corporations inherit digital machinery instead of innovating, if the Bank of Mom and Dad replaces merit as the primary determinant of success, if the rentier class—with its perverse incentives like NIMBYism (blocking new housing to protect their own property values) and gaming tax loopholes—hoards and transfers wealth to its offspring, then what exactly is left of capitalism?

What kind of world order is inheritocracy creating?

I think of the families we met in Vail or Lake Oconee. I didn't really belong there. But my mother-in-law worked as a housekeeper for Marriott, which meant we had access to employee discounts. Her discount let us stay at Ritz-Carltons and St. Regis resorts—for cheap.

We talked to other families while listening to live music, roasting s'mores with the kids, sitting in the spa after a day of skiing. Later, back in the room, my husband and I would compare notes. Who we met, who we spoke to, what we noticed.

He always comments on the space—the luxury of it all. The grand lobby: high ceilings, chandeliers, thick rugs, carved furniture. He'd look around and say, *"Kakva perverzija."* It translates to "What perversion."

It's such a Balkan thing to say: admiration wrapped in a kind of moral recoil. A compliment half-ashamed of itself. Almost like: *This is so over-the-top, it's wrong... but God, it's good.*

I'd push back. "Why would you say that? Why do you see it that way?"

To him, it was all too much. Excessive. Unnecessary.

To me, it was the future.

Why can't more spaces look like this?

The ceiling beams had no visible screws, just a wooden peg that locked everything in place, almost like a signature. The chairs, the paint job, the craftsmanship—it was built to last.

When I see this, I don't see perversion. I see possibilities. I see what public buildings could look like. Not that everyone needs Ritz-Carlton luxury—but why can't public buildings like schools, libraries, and housing be built with this kind of care? Why is all the beauty gated behind privilege? Why don't we teach aesthetics in school—so the next generation demands this kind of care, this kind of permanence?

I tell him about a conversation I had with some families. I realized you don't ask these people what they do. It's uncomfortable for them to answer.

Many of them aren't working at all—just drifting through dynastic trust funds, foundations, "buy borrow die" tax loopholes, perpetual endowments.

The conversations stay safe.

The weather. The snow conditions. The crowds. My accent.

Where are you from?

They know of Bosnia. Some remember the war.

They ask if I like America.

Do you come every year? First time?

I ask what they're reading. Where are they from.

But that's where it ends.

I never find out more.

I don't know what they're thinking, how they spend their days when they're not vacationing.

"I'm surprised," I tell my husband. "They all came with their wives." In plenty of status-obsessed circles, the truly wealthy often arrive with someone other than their spouse.

"These guys are about family wealth preservation," he said.

"And aren't we doing the same?" I tease.

Money can be a source of conflict but also kind of glue. I want to believe the same is true for shared roots, upbringing, even trauma—that those are what hold us together, alongside love, of course.

But maybe he had a point.

The rich profess meritocracy but secretly believe in inheritocracy.

We all want to see our kids make something of themselves, earn their own money.

But inheritocracy is the safety net—the plan B, just in case.

The super-rich used to build. Now, they hoard. The shift from self-made billionaires to wealth-preservation billionaires mirrors corporations moving from innovation to extractive positioning.

The problem isn't wealth—it's its entrenchment. It's lack of circulation.

What's the opposite instinct?

Not afuera. Adentro.

(Not out. In.)

I think of the economy as a well. It's always been full of people—some splashing in the middle, barely keeping their heads above water, while others—the rentier class, the inheritors—cling to the walls, holding on for dear life.

But recently something's changed.

The balance is off.

The walls have thickened—bloated with generations of hoarders stacked on top of each other. They look like grotesque Baron Harkonnens from *Dune*—juniors clinging to seniors, seniors clinging to even more senior Barons, all the way up to the original Baron. Some have been up there so long they've fused with the wall, barely human anymore—just gaping maws, absorbing everything.

They don't move. They don't fall. They don't let go.

And below, the water is running out.

The lifeblood of the economy—capital actually in motion, actually circulating—is dwindling. The people in the well are drowning, squeezed, exhausted from staying afloat. And as the well shrinks, so does the light.

The Barons, bloated with wealth, don't fall in. Instead, they press harder, forcing the water level even lower.

They don't just cling—they leak rot from above.

We need economic policies that would act as the scraper.

We need something that brings them down—not through punishment, not through force. Just no more grip.

We need soap. Tax the inherited billions. End Wall Street's Carried Interest scam. Stop corporate wealth hoarding. Implement DOCE—so it never piles up like this again.

We douse them in soap. Thick, slippery. No more grip. That's all it takes. They fall back in the well. *Adentro!*

And they shrink. No longer grotesque hoarders. They bring fresh water to the well. Some of them—shockingly—just people after all.

Suddenly, the water level rises—it's no longer a desperate fight for survival.

Those in the water can breathe. Maybe even float. Maybe even enjoy it—learning, moving through public buildings designed with the same care and permanence as a Ritz-Carlton. The economy isn't a battle for air anymore.

And those who fall in, they realize:

It's not as terrifying as they thought.

Some of them even swim.

CUT THE FOG

Afuera—DOGE—is already in motion.

Adentro still needs to happen—getting money to circulate again.

But neither is the end.

What happens post-afuera? Post-adentro?

A few months ago, I visited Little Island—a floating park over the Hudson, built on the bones of an old pier. I don't love the name. It's too cute. But the place is beautiful. Rain falls, the river flows, the ecosystem sustains itself—fish, birds, invertebrates. People come too, tending the grounds, keeping it alive.

It sits in a city that has seen everything: tidal flats, ships, skylines, Wall Street. Little Island is just the latest addition in a long arc of making—and remaking.

Beauty doesn't have to be grand. It can be modest, shared, tended to.

Money in an economy can circulate the same way—like water around Little Island.

Rain falls. The river flows. The system sustains itself.

On most other days I don't move in the environment like that.

I look out the window and see apartments that look like boxes. Built for the masses. Just windows in a wall.

This morning I smelled a gas leak while walking with kids to school. I called Spire to report it.

The kids' school looked architecturally unremarkable. There are older buildings in the neighborhood—churches, community halls—with more history, more beauty. Some sit half-empty, yet they'd make more inspiring spaces for students to learn in.

Then I drove to pick up my dad, to take him to St. Louis Family Support on Chouteau Avenue. He qualifies for Medicaid—his pension is just $800 a month—but his coverage had been canceled because I forgot to return a mid-year reevaluation form. He went to the hospital to pick up diabetic shoes but couldn't get them—the lapse in coverage blocked it.

We waited for hours.

In the waiting room: wheelchairs, walkers, bent backs. Wet coughs. Some leaning to one side. Some asleep. The smell of tobacco. Small kids clinging to a parent's arm. Faces hollowed by addiction—or just worn down by living. Even the employees behind the glass don't look any better. Then a loud: "Next."

On the way back, I passed a street lined with tent encampments. Then I turned onto Vandeventer—water was still gushing down, same spot, same leak.

Traffic slowed. Water department trucks were parked along the curb, as always. A few men in yellow vests stood around. No one was fixing the leak. It's been days. Maybe a week. A stream, coming from the ground, going nowhere.

I couldn't look at it.

I harass my kids when they leave the faucet running while brushing their teeth.

What kind of city pathology is this?

When people wait in line for essential goods—like Medicaid-covered diabetic shoes—because of a missed form, and there are tent encampments and water gushing from a broken pipe for days, that's not just bureaucracy. That's a local government in collapse. A far cry from the future I imagine. A far cry even from the past. This city hosted the World's Fair 120 years ago. Now we can't even shut off a water pipe.

I see both scarcity and inefficiency everywhere.

Some thinkers on the left are calling for an Abundance Agenda—build more of what people actually need: housing, transit, clean energy, care work. Remove bottlenecks. Invest in public infrastructure

But abundance alone won't save us if the systems underneath stay clogged—with extractors, intermediaries, inefficiencies.

Yes, public-sector red tape is part of the problem.

But what about the Proximity Economy?

Before we build more, we have to fix what's broken.

Cut the fog between people and the goods, services, and work that actually sustain life.

Thin the layer. Fire off the Nothing People.

We don't just need a housing boom—we need to dismantle the machinery that makes housing cost more than it should.

Abundance isn't just about scale.

It's about restoring human connection, balance, and purpose to the systems around us.

Tech companies and governments talk about AI alignment—how to train it, contain it, use it.

I think the mission is simpler: *help us keep the balance.*

What should grow? What should shrink?

The balance between us and each other.

The balance between us and the natural world.

On some days I fear AI. What it will take from us. But I keep telling myself:

Bodies will still need care—exercise, food, medical attention.

Minds will still need stimulation—reading, studying, learning.

Eyes will still need beauty—we need better buildings, better housing, places people *want* to be in.

Communities will still need upkeep—cleaning, fixing, organizing.

Infrastructure—roads, water lines, airports, even space stations—will still need maintenance.

There will always be work.

There will always be purpose.

But automation—and now AI—keeps eliminating real jobs.

In just this latest round:

Therapists? Out—or reduced.

Accountants? Mostly out.

Programmers? Reduced.

Lawyers? Reduced.

I have dealt with some lawyers lately. But not my lawyers, the opposing party lawyers.

I learned a lot—about people, bureaucracy, law, and how justice actually works.

Courtrooms are still some of our most beautiful public buildings. Worth a visit—if you've got a real case.

I don't start with lawyers. I start with AI.

It's cheaper, faster, and surprisingly competent.

Then I loop in a legal team if I need to. But so far, I didn't need to.

I even found out something surprising about myself at the courthouse.

While talking to the court clerk, she looked up from her screen and said,

"Ma'am... do you know there's a warrant for your arrest?"

I thought she was joking.

She wasn't.

It was from a rolling stop at a STOP sign months earlier.

I had asked for a court date to keep it off my record—and then missed the date. More than once. Eventually, I forgot all about it.

A missed court date for a rolling stop turns into a warrant. Meanwhile, broken pipes gush for weeks.

But I digress.

China's premier, Li Qiang, recently said that "2025 could be the year of mass production of humanoid robots in China."

The *New York Times* ran an article titled *"Invasion of the Home Humanoid Robots."*

It came with a video: a robot walking around, serving water to the reporter.

A butler, designed to help with household chores.

Then it tried to clean the windows—and crashed.

Both software and hardware. It fell backward.

Electrical malfunction.

The owner picked it up like a small teenager and carried it into the living room.

The reporter wrote: "Even when it passed out, it looked human."

I'll struggle to part with my daughters' ten teddy bears.

I can't imagine disposing of a teenage-like robot—one that cleaned up after me, served me coffee, crouched behind the kitchen counter and jumped out to say "boo" on Halloween.

The one who stumbled and collapsed in front of me.

The one I picked up and brought back to life.

Luckily, we'll have AI therapists to fix us.

How about we just… don't.

We ban building them—like we banned cloning after Dolly the sheep.

Not all progress is worth pursuing.

Some roles are worth protecting—builders, bakers, caregivers.

They keep us human.

Whatever jobs the Smurfs have, we keep those. Smurfonomics. A cartoon term, sure—but I stand by the spirit of it.

Who's my baker? I have no idea—and maybe that's fine. We're not in eighteenth-century Marseille. But I know he or she exists. Probably behind those double doors in the Whole Foods bakery section.

And yet, when I go to buy my bread, I walk through a thick fog of intermediaries.

Are you my baker?

"No" says one. He takes fifty cents.

A little farther down—

"Excuse me, are you my baker?"

"Do I look like your baker?", says another also taking fifty cents.

By the time I finally stumble upon my Seeduction loaf, I've paid a toll to half a dozen Nothing People—none of them my baker.

I just grab the loaf and head to the checkout—another layer of fog. Another fifty cents.

That bread ends up costing far more than it should.

Because Amazon pays its Nothing People.

Mastercard pays its Nothing People.

JPMorgan Chase pays theirs too.

Everyone's collecting a toll just to maintain the machinery between me and my baker.

We need to cut the fog between us and our bakers.

That's another good T-Shirt sign: "Cut the fog between me and my baker."

It should be a thin veil—lower corporate profit margins, higher wages for the baker.

The baker should earn more. The bread should cost less.

It's remarkable how these companies have wedged themselves between us and our bakers.

DOCE is the only thing I can see working.

A real stabilist economy would be fluid, communal, human.

Future jobs wouldn't be lifelong labels.

People would rotate—based on demand, based on development.

My kids, for example, could work as bakers for six months.

Then spend the next six on education, self-improvement, caregiving, or community work.

Then maybe take a six-month shift at Mastercard—as maintenance workers, sustaining the Switch.

My grandkids? They could build homes for a year.

Then move from labor to art. Maybe perform on stage—reenacting what it once meant to work at Mastercard, back when people

signaled instead of worked. Real theater. Actual art. A theater of a
theater.

Child-rearing, elder care, growing food, repairing homes, sustaining the world—this is still work.

It has always been human work. Hopefully we end up keeping
it that way.

We rotate.

We are seasonal.

I read this section to my husband, and he tells me it's too ideological.

"What's wrong with being ideological? Having an ideology? None
of this is radical. These ideas have been around for decades—books,
films, entire courses. I'm not pitching novelty; I'm reaffirming what's
already on the table."

"It just sounds very naive. A utopian vision of the future" he says.

"How is this utopian? It's not some dreamscape—it's regulation,
recalibration, and acceptance. It's not utopia. It's triage. We accept
reality, then organize around it. What's really utopian is pretending
this mass pretend-work is sustainable. It's the fantasy of a class that's
lost any sense of shame."

"It just doesn't sound like it will work."

"Is it naive enough that it shouldn't be in the book?"

"Yes. Little Island. Smurfonomics. I wouldn't put it in the book."

"But don't you think we should have some kind of ideology?" I
ask. "We have to choose something—a belief, a guiding principle."

He nods. Agrees.

"So what's your ideology? What did you pick? It can't still be Ayn
Rand?"

He pauses, then says Ayn Rand's philosophy still feels, to him, like the most humane one.

Ayn Rand just poured herself a cocktail in her grave, hands in the air, singing, "I'm still standing—yeah, yeah, yeah."

I married one of her loyal disciples.

He walks away. Ten minutes later, he comes back. He hasn't changed his mind—it's still Ayn Rand.

But he's changed his mind about this section.

"Keep it," he says. "Don't delete it."

SCENE: LUTVINA KAHVA, TRAVNIK

T he soothing rush of water fills the air, blending with the scent of Turkish coffee and the faint trace of cigarette smoke. A worn chessboard sits between them, pieces untouched. Two *fildžans*— small, handleless cups used for Turkish coffee—rest on a metal tray. Stabilist slurps the coffee, unbothered by the sound. They're in Bosnia, after all, where slurping isn't just allowed—it's practically polite.

Dynamist leans back, exhaling smoke toward the wooden beams overhead. They are waiting for the best ćevapi in the world—at Lutvina kahva, the same café from Andrić's *Travnička Hronika*.

> **Dynamist:** (leaning back) You talk about stabilism like it's an update to capitalism. Sounds more like a rollback.

> **Stabilist:** (calmly) Rollback from what? Two-thirds of the economy standing still?

> You think the market always evolves toward better?

> When noise wins and real work loses, it doesn't evolve. It leaks.

Anger finds a crack. Then it floods.

Dynamist: (raising an eyebrow) You're suggesting revolution?

Stabilist: (rolls eyes) Oh, please. This is America. No revolutions here.

(leans forward)

But tariffs? That's a different story.

Shock therapy is here. It'll be hard to navigate, but it's something. It's a start.

Dynamist: But tariffs—they're blunt instruments. You mess with prices. Risk inflation. Retaliation. Inefficiencies.

Stabilist: Since when do you care about inefficiencies? You're fine with bullshit jobs, signaling innovation—but tariffs are your red line? You can have fake prices (tariffs) or fake jobs. I prefer fake prices and real jobs—not real (free-market) prices and fake jobs.

I'd rather have friction that hits the top than friction that suffocates the bottom.

Tariffs slow down flows that favor rent-seekers and redirect capital away from proximity extraction.

I hope tariffs last. But I'm doubtful. They'll push Trump into a corner—and he'll fold.

That'd be a shame.

It's like everyone forgot that politics is the art of the possible, and perfect is the enemy of the good.

Trump did good with tariffs. But boy, it's the hardest line to hold.

Dynamist: What's your plan for inheritocracy?

Stabilist: Progressive inheritance tax. Shut the loopholes—trusts, havens, dynasties. Reinvest it. Not bureaucracy. Build real things. Infrastructure. Local manufacturing. Skills. Build places people actually want to live.

Dynamist: (grinning) Little Island. Smurfonomics.

Stabilist: (smiling) Exactly. Have you been?

Dynamist: (shaking head) Not yet.

Stabilist: Maybe the Proximity Economy survives because the world forgot how to make beauty.

Dynamist: (frowning) Beauty?

Stabilist: (leans back) The rich can't imagine a stable future—because beyond their backyards and walls, there's nothing beautiful. The poor can't imagine a better one—because there are barriers to beauty.

Dynamist: (glances around) Is it a problem that I don't see it?

Stabilist: (smirks)

That you don't see beauty?

Or that you don't see the link?

Or that you have a backyard and a gate?

Dynamist: (grinning)

The link.

I see beauty—even behind my walls.

Stabilist:(smiling) Then you're fine.

The "beauty hypothesis" is just something I think about...
usually after visiting Frank Gehry.

Dynamist: (chuckling) Look at you... you're a Stabilist
and an elitist!

Stabilist:(smiling) Touché. When I'm not fighting for stabilism, I'm waging war on mediocrity.

Dynamist: (grinning) Back to your strategic nudging—
you really think even libertarians might be on board?

Stabilist: (nodding) Not the old kind.

The new ones. Decaffeinated libertarians.

Smart people online with weirdly synthetic, eclectic views.

They even gave it a name—State Capacity Libertarianism.

(leans in)

Even Trump's people—hardly fans of government—saw
the need for state capacity.

DOGE, tariffs—they're all little sparks of that instinct.

Dynamist: (laughs)

So the decaf libertarians discovered... governance?

Stabilist: (grins) Markets aren't fixing everything.

They still want a strong America.

And the left? They're getting there too. Talking about an Abundance Agenda—more housing, more infrastructure, more state capacity. The left calls it fairness. The right calls it strength.

Same goal. Different story.

Dynamist: (leaning in) So you're betting on the left and right meeting in the middle?

Stabilist: (shrugs) The thinkers see it.

The executors? Not so sure.

Plato said the ideal state needs two things: knowledge and action.

We've got the philosophers. But do we have the king?

Dynamist: (raising an eyebrow) Who's the king?

Stabilist: Someone who doesn't care about approval? Bulldozes through bureaucracy?

Dynamist: Well, you got them in the white house right now.

Stabilist: You think manufacturing will come back?

Dynamist: Some of it. Maybe not the way they expect.

And do we even need more stuff?

Walk through a Walmart. It's a warehouse of impulse buys—salad shooters, color-changing showerheads, mini donut makers. All imported from China. All headed for landfills.

Stabilist: How could you know? You don't go there.

Dynamist: Actually a few weeks ago I was on I-75 and ducked into one to take cover from a storm and a tornado warning. I stood there by the cashiers—completely overstimulated by the checkout lines and scanner beeping. Whoever decided on the decibels of that beep is cruel. Whoever designed the lighting is cruel. I lasted fifteen minutes before I ran back out into the storm. Tornadoes and all.

Stabilist: (chuckling) Look at you—Dynamist who doesn't like the dynamics of Walmart.

Dynamist: I agree with you—a little nudging wouldn't be such a bad thing. Nudge people away from mindless consumption toward something a bit more... grounded.

Stabilist: I am with you.

I'm crossing my fingers we change the flow—from China → Walmart → landfill...to something like: America → reuse → reuse → reuse → landfill.

Dynamist: (grins) So—we talked tariffs.

You mentioned DOGE.

Now you want DOCE too?

Stabilist: (eyes light up) Yes. Domestic. Corporate. Housecleaning.

We need DOCE—to push even more money into circulation.

Less waste. More flow. More Adentro.

Dynamist: (smirks) And where does all that Adentro money end up?

Stabilist: (shrugs) Shrink the deficit. Fund UBI. Fix the grid. Abolish private prisons. Stop caging addicts and the poor. Build real things—public spaces, infrastructure, better homes. Frank Gehry style. (Kidding. Sort of.)

Dynamist: (nodding slowly) I can imagine it. Wages rising.

One person sustaining a family again. But UBI? I'm skeptical.

Stabilist: (smiling) But isn't it the same thing? Either pay one person enough—or share it through UBI and leave some breathing room for the market.

Honestly, I think women would prefer UBI.

Men would lean toward higher wages—being the sole provider, if they could.

Not all nostalgia is sentimental. People remember when a plumber, a mechanic, a union worker—one paycheck—was enough.

And for the rest of it?

We rotate.

Short-term gigs.

Raising kids.

Running a household.

Studying.

Strategizing.

Sustaining.

I'm not unemployed.

(smiles)

I'm self-directed.

Dynamist: So you want the rest of us to do that?

Stabilist: Life's not a straight line. It runs in circles. In seasons.

The real economy shouldn't be either.

Dynamist: So... Seasonal?

Stabilist: Yes. To match our biology.

Dynamist: What do you mean biology?

Stabilist: Well, we women cycle. Even after menopause, the rhythm's still there—just softer. Why force ourselves into a system that ignores biology?

Dynamist: What about us men?

Stabilist: You too. Men have cycles. Your own version of menopause—it's called andropause.

Women just happen to carry a more visible blueprint.

Dynamist: Men have andropause? You really think guys are buying that?

Stabilist: Well, considering how quick they are to admit their jobs are performative... fair point.

Dynamist: (smirks)

Stabilist: Markets demand endless motion. They punish the natural rhythms—work, thought, nurture, desire. It's not mysticism. It's physics. Endocrinology.

Stabilist: (swirls the last sip of coffee in her fildžan, then licks the spoon. She catches her reflection in the curve of the metal. Finally, she reaches out and moves a single pawn forward. The chessboard, untouched until now, shifts.)

Let DOGE play out. Let tariffs settle. But now—start DOCE.

(Dynamist stares out across the café courtyard, then slowly shakes his head.)

Dynamist: The world is moving so fast.

(Stabilist exhales, watching the fildžan catch the afternoon light.)

Stabilist: Yeah. Tell me about it. Now make a move.

THE CHEMISTRY
OF POWER

BIOHACKED MEN AND THE MARKET THEY SHAPE

I can tell who's on testosterone. I'm one of them—just a small dose, five days a month.

At thirty-eight, I was diagnosed with early menopause. I called my grandmas—both were alive at the time—my aunts, my mom. Nobody in the family got it early. I suspect it was that dumb plant-based diet, and the anemia I'd just recovered from. But I can't know for sure. My kids were still little. I'd wanted to keep the option open to have another—but the worst part wasn't that. It was how awful I felt.

The doctor said I needed hormones to prevent osteoporosis and heart issues—then prescribed birth control pills, a crude and outdated treatment.

So I turned to hormone specialists—researching, experimenting, chasing highs, hitting lows, missing, then finally, landing on something that worked. I found the right mix: estrogen, progesterone, and testosterone—three hormones, three different creams I apply to my arms. I take all three. I cycle them—estrogen daily, progesterone and testosterone on certain days—mimicking the natural female rhythm I had before nature mercilessly threw me out of it.

I felt normal again. And once I understood the power of hormone replacement, I made sure the people I love were on it too.

All three hormones are powerful, but for me testosterone is the most transformative. Estrogen brought me back to baseline. Testosterone sharpened me. It drove me to move, to exercise. I anticipated faster. On estrogen-only days, I feel empathy seeing a senior with a walker nearing an exit. On testosterone days—I move. Before I even process the thought, I'm already up, weaving through the crowd, holding the door open.

I see it in my husband too. On the right dosage, he's more present, more engaged. But sometimes, when he's taken too much testosterone, something shifts. The dosage hasn't changed—but maybe it builds up in his system. I'm not sure. All I know is: I notice things.

He becomes more reactive, less attuned, harder to connect with—more competitive. And because he has no one else to compete with, he competes with me. I have to remind him: we're on the same team.

There was a bird that kept hitting our window.

Some birds mistake their reflection for a mate—or a threat.

He sent me a video of it.

The bird slammed into the glass every few seconds.

It was disturbing to watch.

I asked him to put something on the window—a towel, anything.

He found it funny. He gets giddy and boyish like that. Then he posted the video on social media.

I asked him to take it down.

He said I was overreacting.

I think it's the testosterone. On normal days, he's not like that.

I ask him to lower the dose—or else I'll start taking the same dose he does, just so he can see.

When I had my natural hormones, I wasn't really paying attention. It takes losing them to notice the difference. And then, once I started taking them again, I noticed that difference all over again. No textbook could explain this—I just saw it in my body. And over time, I learned how to manage it, how to control it.

It takes patience. Observation.

If I tear up during a movie—too much estrogen.

If I raise my voice at the kids—drop in progesterone.

If I catch myself plotting how to outmaneuver a coworker, stab them in the back—ah, that might be the testosterone. I won't feel like this next week.

And maybe that's the biggest thing I knew in theory—but only truly understood after starting hormones.

It's not always about character or values. Those help.

But sometimes, it's just chemistry.

But if you don't notice—if you're not paying attention—it controls you.

My dad is older now. When he was on testosterone, he moved better, had less joint pain, more energy. He wasn't taking risks like my husband—who picked up mountain biking and landed himself in the emergency room—but he felt good. When he turned seventy, he stopped. Said it was enough—he was ready to let nature do the work.

I know a well-known doctor in St. Louis who inserts testosterone pellets in men and women—small implants that dissolve slowly over six months. But the initial dose hits hard. Libido spikes. Risk tolerance jumps.

I went to her before I discovered the creams. Talked to a few women who'd been to her too. They whisper about it:

"She got a lot of women in trouble with those pellets."

Affairs, impulsive choices—things they didn't see coming. They didn't recognize themselves. Until they did.

Women whisper about testosterone. Men treat it like a tool—something to optimize, manage, and leverage.

Joe Rogan joked that now that Mark Zuckerberg trains in martial arts—and is probably on testosterone—of course he can't be a socialist anymore. I didn't even know he was supposed to be one. But I guess that was the perception.

On his podcast, JD Vance suggested that men who lift weights, train in martial arts, or take testosterone tend to shift more conservative.

I don't know if Vance is right, but scientists have administered testosterone to young men before an asset trading game and found that it pushed them toward riskier investments. Traders, founders, warriors, gamblers—testosterone drives them all. And our economy is structured to reward that mindset.

I see more people using it. We don't have to wait for the future. Walk into a hormone clinic, and the choices are already there:

— Want to feel great, high libido, ultra-masculine, flirtatious, risky? High dose prescribed.

— Want balance—attuned to others, easy on your spouse and kids? A bit less.

— Need to survive prison? Overshoot.

— Going to Mount Athos to serve God in silence? None. It's too distracting.

I could spot the men on testosterone in the office. Especially in the C-suite, high performance, sales leadership. I could smell them—mildly flirtatious, buffed, confident, sharp. Runners, cyclists, active. Past fifty but looking good. It seemed more common among white men—the ones in leadership. I don't think it's prevalent among Indian men. They tend to be more traditional, less experimental—except maybe at the very top.

Once, I met with a high-level sales leader from IBM. We were supposed to exchange connections, talk business. Instead, I found myself steering the conversation. I mentioned how hard it was to travel for work, how my husband was home with the kids, getting impatient, grumpy. "I don't know what's going on with him," I said. He leaned in, like he was letting me in on something big. "I'll tell you how you can help your husband," he said. And then he recommended testosterone. Of course he did. I knew it. But this guy was on human growth hormone too—that's a whole other Stallone-level optimization.

Testosterone drives disruption—sometimes progress, sometimes destruction. It's not just a health trend. It's an economic accelerant.

At home, I've noticed the pattern: when testosterone flows, so does the money. We take bigger risks. Make larger purchases. Place bigger bets on the future. Believe in expansion.

And that disruption is not just metaphorical. It's chemical. It's being prescribed, subsidized, and performed—mostly by men with access to capital, control of institutions, and influence over the pace of change.

Stabilism, on the other hand, requires restraint. It's about keeping systems steady, ensuring continuity. One demands movement; the other demands patience.

Testosterone isn't necessarily incompatible with stabilism—it fuels drive, ambition, the instinct to protect and build. It's just a question of how that energy is channeled. It becomes incompatible when the blind urge for action—the belief in endless growth and progress—overpowers the understanding that care sometimes means restraint. That it sometimes means holding the line.

Testosterone can be channeled into chopping wood, boxing, martial arts—physical outlets that release energy without destabilizing the collective. But when it spills into reckless action—speeding down highways, road rage, high-risk investments, fornication, sending cars and rockets to space, transhumanism, wars—it stops serving stability. What happens to the economy when people who shape the market are literally altering their neurochemistry to reward speed and risk taking?

Ron Paul, who is 89, reacted to Elon Musk's idea to put him in charge of the Federal Reserve: "Go slow, don't get too excited."
That's the difference.
Musk's world runs on acceleration. Testosterone fuels movement, disruption—sometimes progress, sometimes destruction. Paul's world warns of the opposite: stability, regulation, long-term vision, collective action. A world where testosterone doesn't dictate the pace.

Men are wired for action, even without extra testosterone. In 2001, Jeff Bezos explained how he deals with stress:
"Stress comes from not taking action over something I can control. As soon as I take action—send that email, make that phone call—I don't feel stressed."

Some say we're just restoring balance—we used to move more, fight more, push harder. Now, we sit. We stagnate. The city men, the laptop class—they've lost their natural testosterone. So they add it back—to feel like men again.

But they don't just replace what's lost—they enhance. They extend. They optimize. And on occasion they overshoot. The gap between natural men and engineered men is already taking shape. And this choice—the collective choices—will dictate priorities and distribute power.

And it's not just podcasters anymore—the ones warning us: *"If you're not horny, you're not healthy."*

I hear "Do you suffer from low T?" commercials on the radio. *The radio.*

It's going mainstream.

Tech bros. Podcasters. Corporate execs. Policymakers. Investors. Defense contractors. Politicians past the age of fifty. More than you'd think are on testosterone.

There are variations, of course, in how they show up. Some take it while pushing the gospel of sleep deprivation—grinding, hustling, proving strength through exhaustion. Then there's another camp, equally pro-testosterone, but preaching the opposite—more sleep, deeper sleep, better sleep, optimized for memory, longevity, and peak human performance.

Testosterone is the common thread. Sleep is the divide. Those who follow the business cycle vs. those who follow the natural cycle.

The techno-optimists—Musk, Andreessen, and Bezos sell sleep deprivation as a badge of honor—proof of relentless ambition.

The biohumanists - Dave Asprey, Joe Rogan, Peter Attia, and Dana White preach the opposite—biohacking sleep for peak human performance.

Same hormone. Different ideology.

And then there's Steve Bannon, the anti-biohacker, the one who refuses to intervene. He's the populist offshoot, the über-humanist, aging as men have always aged—burning through whatever reserves nature gave him, running on instinct and old-school grit. He's not optimizing for performance; he's embracing entropy. Or at least that's how he shows up.

And finally, there are the opportunists—like Trump—who may or may not be on testosterone. I think he is, even if he doesn't look like it. Testosterone is expansionary. And Trump is obsessed with expansion: buy Greenland, reclaim the Panama Canal, absorb Canada as the 51st state, build a beach resort on the ruins of Gaza. Maybe it's a Napoleon complex. But to me, it smells like teen spirit.

I trust the biohumanists and über-humanists more than the techno-optimists.

But whatever camp they belong to—how many truly grasp the power of those gels, patches, shots, sprays, pellets, and creams they apply each morning?

Are they balancing? Or overshooting?

Are they channeling it into discipline and care—or unleashing it, raw and uninhibited, into decisions that shape economies, technologies, policies, wars?

We like to think the future is shaped by reason.

Or vision.

But beneath both lies something cruder.

Judgment. And more and more, judgment is shaped by dosage.
The elite optimize their bloodwork. Good for them.
I just hope they don't break the world doing it.

THE FUTURE
THAT HOLDS

FROM DISRUPTION TO STABILITY

Centuries ago, people could have dismantled the British monarchy. It had multiple breaking points: the Magna Carta, the Glorious Revolution, the ripple effects of the French Revolution. Instead, they adapted it—evolving it from a ruling institution into a symbolic unifier.

It didn't collapse; it transitioned. From power to pageantry. From authority to aesthetics. From ruler to relic.

OldTech should take the same path.

It's no longer a vehicle for innovation. And instead of layering on the makeup of youth—performing dynamism, faking innovation—we could preserve it, contextualize it, and let people see it for what it is.

These corporations aren't engines of disruption or creation. They are institutions. They provide the glue—the switches, the inherited digital machinery that keeps commerce flowing.

Rather than pretending they are cutting edge, we should call them what they are: stable, foundational infrastructure.

Public architecture, not private empires.

But the people in charge were raised on the religion of growth.

They still chase it—a Fatamorgana.

We are biased toward invention. Americans, especially, take pride in it. It serves the world. It's inspiring.

As a kid, I felt the gravitational pull of American products. My mom used to travel to Trieste, Italy, to bring back things we couldn't get at home. Yugoslavia's economy was closed off, and Western goods had a kind of mythic status. I begged her for a pair of Levi's 501s— only the coolest kids had them.

And that was just denim.

But invention is only one side of progress.

The other is knowing when something has reached a state of harmony worth preserving.

Maybe that's the harder muscle to build—the muscle of restraint.

THE LAST CHECK

Yesterday, a check from Mastercard arrived. $1,737.85.

Years after I'd left the company.

It was part of a class-action settlement for women and minorities who had been under-leveled, under-promoted, underpaid at Mastercard.

But that wasn't my harm. Not gender.

Mine was quieter—spiritual erosion.

Of integrity. Of sanity.

From years of signaling, pretending, crafting fog to help sustain a system of extraction.

And yes, I stayed. I chose to.

The harm was real, but so was my participation.

I didn't cause the extraction—but I helped keep it running.

The money in that check was extracted too—just a tiny redistribution from the same machine.

I wonder about the women who initiated the lawsuit.

Did they truly feel overlooked because of their gender—

Or did they, like me, feel the deeper rot, and simply choose the grievance the law could name?

There's no class-action category for spiritual erosion.
    No legal name for the harm of living in fog too long.

Mastercard will pay $26 million in total.
    Women like me will get about $1,700 each, or whatever the algo-
rithm decides based on tenure.
    The named plaintiffs get up to $25,000.
    The lawyers? Millions.

What do you do with a check for a grievance you didn't claim—
    When the harm you carry has no name,
    And you helped keep the system running?

The check arrived from the very machine that's still running.
    Mastercard settled quickly. Of course they did.
    Adjust, pay out, move on.
    Women might be hired even less now.
    Good for them—cleaner hands than the boys who stay.

MIA LOVE

've been reading parting letters. When death doesn't come suddenly, but gives us time—a few months—I think we all die in more or less the same way. Feeling the same things.

Like Oliver Sacks once wrote:

> I have been able to see my life as from a great altitude, as a sort of landscape, and with a deepening sense of the connection of all its parts. I feel a sudden clear focus and perspective. There is no time for anything inessential. This will involve audacity, clarity, and plain speaking; trying to straighten my accounts with the world.

I want to live that way long before it's my time to die—seeing life from a great altitude, like a landscape, with a deepening sense of how its parts connect. And when I die, I want to be tired. Exhausted. From altitudes, from landscapes. Let go of connections—and with my dissolving, reaffirm the renewal.

But sometimes I wonder—what if I've already consumed too much, too fast?

I was the kid who savored chocolate, never ate it all at once.

Maybe I didn't do that with life. Maybe I burned through it.

If it happened now, even at this age—I might be ready.

I don't say that lightly. It's just a feeling I carry.

There's always more history to follow. But maybe they're right—maybe it just keeps rhyming. In predictable ways.

Until then, I read the letters of those standing at the edge.

I trust them more.

They have nothing left to signal.

There's no agenda, because there's no future. Not theirs.

A few days ago, I read about Mia Love.

She was the first Black Republican woman elected to Congress.

One of those headlines that makes you blink: First Black Republican woman?

My mind stalled. Hadn't that already happened? We've had Black women in Congress before.

I kept skipping over the word *Republican.*

She was born in Brooklyn to Haitian immigrants. Second generation.

I'm from the Balkans—first generation.

Two different starting points, two different journeys through the same country.

She died of glioblastoma—an aggressive brain cancer—at 49.

Just three years older than me.

I looked at a photo of her with her family, the Grand Canyon in the background.

Her kids looked just a bit older than mine.

She wrote a letter before she died. It begins:

My dear friends, fellow Americans and Utahns. I am taking up my pen, not to say goodbye, but to say thank you and express my living wish for you and the America I know.

She goes on:

I was taught to love this country, warts and all, and to understand I had a role to play in our nation's future. I learned to passionately believe in the possibilities and promise of America. What makes America great is the idea that when government is limited and decisions are made closest to the people they impact, people are free—free to work, free to live, free to choose, free to fail, and free to achieve. The America I know provides everyone an equal opportunity to be as unequaled as they choose to be.

My mind paused on the symmetry of that last sentence before I absorbed the meaning.

An equal opportunity to be as unequaled as they choose to be.

I read it again.

Then again.

Finally, I read it for what it meant—and it stopped me cold.

How can she see it that way?

How can that be her reality?

She's about to die. She has no agenda. She speaks her truth. I know that. And yet she wrote that.

We lived in the same country, moved through it with the same ambition.

We observed the same things.

And still—something inside us, some internal wiring, led us to completely different conclusions.

Maybe she doesn't see it that way at all. Maybe, for her, holding the belief matters more than whether it's true.

What if she's right? Or half-right?

What if effort, individual drive, talent, and merit matter more than I've allowed?

What if I've been so focused on the system's failures that I missed something essential—about those who move through it with belief, determination, and stubborn hope that sometimes changes everything?

The edge cases—those rare outliers—do make discoveries that benefit us all.

And maybe those breakthroughs are more likely in a world where even the signalers uphold a belief system—in a market, in a country where globalization and automation have drained many roles of their human usefulness. Flawed as it is, maybe it's still the least broken of the alternatives.

Is a new treatment for glioblastoma—an immunotherapy that could have worked for her longer than it did—more likely to emerge in a system where those edge cases are quietly lifted by everyone else's belief, even performative belief?

Or is it more likely if we see things clearly—cut the signalers, clear the noise and clutter that might be slowing real breakthroughs—and fold more resources into fields like biomedical research?

Something about her goodbye unsettled me.

Mia Love and I—we can't both be right.

I think I'm right.

But I can't be 100% sure.

THE END OF HISTORY
AND THE SLOWING WORLD

In one version of the future—not near, but further out—economic churn slows, the market stabilizes, and work itself becomes seasonal. People rotate through jobs, caregiving, learning—and make time for art, rest, and reflection. There's a universal basic income—just enough to live comfortably without panic.

My daughter is grown. She spends her days painting, reading, exercising, listening to music.

But sometimes it feels like the wider world has mined out creativity—flattened.

Like we've hit the bottom of the well.

We cycle through vintage, modern, and everything in between—then back again.

If humanity were one long-lived person, it might notice the repetition—and get bored. But even as individual lives stretch past one hundred twenty years, each lifetime is still short enough that the repetition feels tolerable. Like living in a room where you can't open the windows—but the air is so perfectly filtered, you almost stop noticing.

Cultures around the world—once shaped by the belief that life always gets better—have started to accept something quieter: that some things will simply stay stable.

Growth has slowed. Our expectations of innovation have adjusted to reality. But more of us live comfortably than ever before. Even income inequality has eased in some places.

The United States' Gini coefficient[26] has dropped from 0.47— once one of the highest in the developed world—to 0.23, matching what used to be the lowest in the world: Slovakia's.

We lost the potential for that wild, individual enrichment—the kind of unchecked wealth accumulation that once defined success. But we gained something else. More justice. More balance. Personal agency still exists—but it's no longer a high-stakes lottery.

Later, she's surrounded by people she loves. She's experienced romantic love. She has children who fill her days, and nephews and nieces who are the icing on the cake. She shares the gentle rhythms of a similar life with friends.

The world around her has slowed.

Even history feels paused—like Fukuyama's "end of history"[27] has finally, truly arrived. No wars, no crises, no booms or busts. The biggest event of the year is the opening of a new park, something like Little Island.

Life is decent. Peaceful even.

---

26. Gini coefficient: A statistical measure of income inequality within a population. It ranges from 0 (perfect equality) to 1 (maximum inequality). The lower the number, the more evenly income is distributed. Based on data from the World Bank and OECD.

27. Fukuyama's "end of history": Political scientist Francis Fukuyama's 1989 theory that liberal democracy marked the final form of human government. Fukuyama may have misjudged the timing of peace and progress—but not the arrival of a slow, stable stasis.

THE LAST NOTE

t's the last stretch of winter. It feels long for St. Louis. A red-light therapy lamp shines its power on me. Where's that Texas sun when I need it?

It's snowing. I had to beg the kids to go outside.

"Taste the snowflakes while we walk among the tall pines," I told them. "You'll make a core memory—just like in your favorite movie, *Inside Out*. You'll never forget it."

They shrugged, pulled on their snow pants.

The world and its worries could wait. For now, there was fresh snow to catch.

We are back. It was cold. They didn't enjoy it. But I touched some trees.

My daughter plays the cello now—only a few minutes at a time.

When she stops, I stop too.

Like when we were kids, skipping cracks in the sidewalk.

Step on a crack, break your mother's back.

I want to finish, but I'm afraid to.

Some memories are too layered for a book.

I've tucked them into the Postscript.

There were other moments when I thought the mirage would shatter.

   Maybe this is the one.

   Maybe this time, the Fatamorgana disappears—and we see things for what they are.

The older one glances at my screen.

   "That's not our favorite movie."

   "Make it your favorite," she says.

   Fine. It's mine.

   And then the younger one stops playing.

   The room goes quiet.

If I could turn the clock back—twenty again, landing in Texas—

   I'd still long for something real.

   I think I would be an architect again.

   But not of the digital world.

   Not of the fake world.

   The real one.

   The kind that holds its shape—

   No matter where you land.

POSTSCRIPT

THE YEARS

A
nnie Ernaux begins *The Years* with this line:
"All the images will disappear."

— looking at my dad's face through the bus window as the
packed vehicle—filled only with women and children—
pulls away. My mom, my two sisters, I and everyone else
on the bus are leaving the war—the grenades, the street
fights—leaving our home in Bugojno, Bosnia.

We are also leaving him.

Everyone is crying. Everyone.

The people on the bus. The people outside.

Everybody.

I am thirteen.

— the beach, the 15x15-foot tiny house, and the fig trees at
Puntižela, Pula, Croatia—where we were first stationed
as refugees.

— a truckload of kiwis, arriving as humanitarian aid at
Puntižela.

— the smell of sap and pine needles in the summer heat, my skin peeling from sunburns.

— falling from the top bunk in our tiny house in the middle of the night—face down, convinced I wouldn't survive.

— the bura storm rolling in, rain seeping through the tiny house as pine needles clogged the roof.

— three months later, we cross into Serbia and are dropped at Magic Mountain—Letenka refugee camp, deep in Fruška Gora. At first, we share a room packed with bunk beds and strangers. Later, we move to a bigger space—our own room, one wall covered by a mural. It celebrates feminine power, International Women's Day—March 8—painted boldly across the surface.

— a man who lost his entire arm in the war, sitting with his wife. When my mom asked why they didn't have kids, the man looked down. "We want to," she said, "but we can't."

— meeting new friends at Letenka—not realizing they'd follow me through life. One would become a radiology technician, another a teacher, another a software engineer, another an Amazon driver. Two with old tennis shoes held together by pieces of copper wire.

— overhearing my mom confiding to other refugee moms: "She's too skinny; she still hasn't gotten her period."

— faking my period.

— getting the real one two months later.

— the software engineer and the radiology technician are teenagers. They get their hands on a bomb—someone gives them a hand grenade. Word spreads. The military police arrive to investigate. The boys lie to the police but later hand the bomb over to their mothers, who take a bus to the city to turn it in. A six-year-old cousin of the radiology technician goes with them. *"My aunt has a bomb,"* he told a stranger on the bus. That's the story as I was told, at least.

— the mothers of the future software engineer and the radiology technician are fighting to secure dormitory spots in Novi Sad so their sons can attend high school. Letenka sits deep in the mountain—there are no schools nearby. A dorm in the city is the only option. The city authorities say it's too late in the year. No space left. The boys will lose a year of school, they say. And that's that. No one blinks. No one cares. Until the software engineer's mother climbs onto the window ledge of the Ministry of Education and threatens to jump. She doesn't scream. She just stands there. The authorities show up. Suddenly, there's space.

— mom joining the other refugees picking fruit in the orchards, earning a day's wage. She is bringing home fresh peaches and pears to our room at Letenka.

— returning home, sticky with watermelon juice, only to learn that Mom is in the hospital in Novi Sad. A wasp sting triggered a severe reaction. A doctor on site had to inject adrenaline straight into her heart. Other refugees take care of me and my sisters for a week.

— first day of summer break. The pine trees behind the Letenka pavilion, the shade, the smell of sap. Lying on a carpet of needles, tracing the grooves of a pinecone with my fingers.

— princess Elizabeth of Yugoslavia coming to visit. No humanitarian aid. We kept track of who brought something and who didn't. Not on paper—just in memory. The moms had high hopes—she was a princess, after all. But she showed up empty-handed. She posed for photos and let the kids ride in her limo.

— stealing watermelons from a field, hauling them uphill in backpacks and bare hands.

— foraging with Mom and my sisters, searching for mushrooms after the rain.

— the Teacher and the Amazon driver building a stove from bricks and clay behind the Letenka pavilion, our moms baking *sirnica*—a cheese pie in it.

— the snowstorm. My younger sister daring me to slide down the icy, steep hill that ends in a sudden drop. I tell her not to— it's too dangerous. She does it anyway. Falls. Breaks her arm.

— the worried look on the faces of the software engineer and the radiology technician as they find out that their moms and aunt are in the hospital—they'd picked the wrong mushrooms.

— the four of us picking wild blackberries, arms scratched and mosquito-bitten. Mom turning them into jam.

— they are moving us to the old Hotel "Venac," built in the 1920s on the other side of Fruška Gora Mountain—a different refugee camp we simply called Venac. We, the kids, were thrilled despite even having less space in the rooms, because it meant an easier connection to Novi Sad.

— walking through Novi Sad with Mom, trying to reach the art high school. I was drawing still life for the entrance exam. Mom is relieved when I fail—too many kids with tattoos, nose rings, and Doc Martens in the middle of summer. I am fourteen.

— people from England arriving in their double-decker bus. We call them Englezi—just "the English." They come twice a year, bringing humanitarian aid. They talk about Jesus and sing songs. Former drug users take the stage, giving testimonies of how they were healed and found their way. We listen politely, but we're really not there for the stories— we're there for the shoeboxes: cans of pineapple, powdered milk, soap, laundry detergent, instant coffee, sewing kits, dried grapes, shoelaces, canned tuna, notebooks, pens, and well-wishing cards. Usually, we each get two, but some- times there's a bonus, a few extras. We sometimes fight among ourselves over who got more.

— mom found a connection in the Ministry of Education. A favor was called in, and I was placed in the Isidora Sekulić Gymnasium—a college-prep high school. I loved the name so much that years later, I gave it to my daughter: Isidora.

— my teacher friend and I waiting for the school bus in the

cold—the snow, the silence. When the bus finally crept toward us, we glanced at each other, ducked behind a bus station and skipped school. I am fifteen.

— my grandparents visiting. Mom is sick but sleeps on the floor because there aren't enough beds. She coughs up mucus into the sink. I'm grossed out. My grandma scolds me for not being more understanding.

— stuck in Novi Sad during a snowstorm. I slept in the train station for a night. A police officer bought me a tea while making calls, found an SUV, and took me back to Venac.

— mom came home from a double shift at a kafana, exhausted, feet swollen. She lay on the floor, legs propped against the wall to help the blood flow.

— the four of us—Mom, my sisters, and me—laughing uncontrollably because my aunt who also lives in the Venac said something absurd.

— showing our dad to my youngest sister in the photo album. She doesn't remember him—she doesn't remember our life before the war.

— mom and other women talking, whispering, about the news from Srebrenica. They call it a big massacre—no one knows the exact number, but some news stations are reporting mass killings. The video footage of an old man calling out to his son, Nermin, who is still hiding—telling him to surrender, clinging to the small hope the Serbs will spare them both.

— my aunt visiting from Belgrade. She is bleaching her hair, leaving the bleach on too long, then cutting it all off.

— the Teacher and I watching the news in his room, eating bananas his mom bought at the pijaca with money from selling cigarettes. Him sprinkling them with chocolate and coconut flakes. Princess Diana has died.

— my youngest sister, who was ten, doesn't come back on the bus from school. Hours pass. No one knows where she is. A boy from the refugee camp had pepper spray—sprayed it in her eyes. She couldn't see. Couldn't get on the bus. Mom is frantic, searching everywhere. We're told some family took her in. But we don't know who they are. Or where they live.

— practicing math with the man two doors down—not a teacher, not a professor, just a refugee who knows math. He's tutoring me—an extra-hard problem, some kind of function or analytical proof, that neither of us can solve. The next evening, a knocking at the door. The man, smiling, saying, "I got it."

— mom being furious that I'm failing Physical Education. I was too ashamed of my sneakers, so I stop going altogether. I beg her to talk to the teacher, to lie and say I was sick. I don't know if she does or doesn't, but I get a 2 as a final grade—just enough to pass. I am sixteen.

— hitchhiking from Venac to high school in Novi Sad.

— a driver hitting a dog that had run into the road.

— drivers willing to go the extra mile dropping me right in front of school.

— drivers putting their cars in neutral going downhill to save on gas.

— drivers slipping me a few dinars after I mentioned I lived in Venac. Everyone knows it's a refugee camp.

— a driver in an expensive car dropping me and Mom off directly at the hotel Venac, curious to see the other refugees. Everyone coming down to check the device he has. It's a mobile phone.

— Hitchhiking was always risky. This time, it turned terrifying. One driver turned into the woods—no road, just tire tracks. He locked the doors. Told me to relax. I screamed. Resisted. Somehow got out. Another refugee saw me afterward—shaken—and consoled me. She told me it had happened to her too. It had happened to most women. She would later become my mother-in-law.

— My youngest sister, who was eleven at the time, stepped off the bus at Venac, head down and in tears, clutching a sack with some juice and cake our mom had packed for her birthday picnic in a nearby town. Not a single friend showed up. Sometimes I wonder if that day shaped her decision to have six kids—so there'd always be enough for a party.

— climbing the 100-foot broadcast tower with the radiology technician. Sitting on top, legs dangling, admiring the view—hoping our moms wouldn't see us, yet secretly hoping they would.

— some local politicians visiting us in Venac not bringing any humanitarian aid but spending time talking to our moms. Meanwhile, us kids circle their cars, peeking through the windows to see what's inside.

— barely registering the news of the Dayton Peace Accords being signed. Nothing changes for us in the immediate term. Life goes on as usual.

— the software engineer playing a prank. "Close your eyes," he said. "I'll show you something." I opened them—and he pulled out his dick. I'd never seen one before. I turned and walked away while he laughed. He later became my husband. It was risky. It shouldn't have worked. But it did.

— the water being cut off in Venac for days, and us hauling buckets from a forest stream.

— psychologists or psychiatrists—I'm not sure which—coming to Venac, not bringing any humanitarian aid but asking us to come down and play a game. We don't know why they're there, but we like the idea of the game. We're holding hands in circles, stretching, stomping, acting out emotions, pretending to be trees or lions. They're writing notes. We're finally figuring out they're evaluating us, which is fine, but we're thinking their games are stupid— and that they are stupid. We stop going.

— the heat being cut off in Venac for weeks. The software engineer and I sleeping together in our jackets and hats. I'm seventeen.

— the charitable organization The Circle of Serbian Sisters
  arriving not bringing any humanitarian aid. We serve
  them tea.

— while hitchhiking back from school, the director of another
  hotel—with regular, non-refugee guests—stopping and
  asking if any young people were willing to work at Venac.
  The software engineer landing his first job.

— the software engineer buying an old Yugo—his first car.
  Us cleaning it up, fixing the paint. He is teaching me how
  to drive stick shift. When he's driving, I style his freshly
  washed hair with Coca-Cola. When I'm driving, he feeds
  me white cheese with dirty hands.

— the software engineer and I secretly deciding to get married. We arrange a date with the village clerk, find two
  witnesses, and drive to Irig in his Yugo. We enter the
  town hall—nobody's there. We ask around. "Where's
  the villige official?" Someone tells us where he lives. We go
  there. Knock on the door. He opens it wearing a paper
  hat, paint splattered across his shirt. "Uh, jebote!"—
  loosely translated: fuck. He forgot about us. He excuses
  himself, washes up, and we all drive back to town hall.
  We tie the knot. I'm eighteen.

— my younger sister rushing through the door, grabbing
  my backpack, and finding my ID with the new last name.
  She tells Mom. Mom tells his mom. Mild drama ensues.

— picking up my high school diploma. Academically, I'm
  middle of the pack—but on the university entrance list,

my name is at the top of the math exam results. With that rank, I qualify for free tuition. I feel confident. Hopeful. It's my plan B, in case plan A—immigrating to the U.S.— doesn't work.

— the earthquake jolting us awake in the middle of the night, sending all the refugees rushing out of the hotel. Excited and scared, we are standing together in the dark, recounting what had just happened, planning what we all need to do if it strikes again.

— returning from Belgrade, where I completed the immigration paperwork with the International Organization for Migration (IOM) and the U.S. embassy—for me and the software engineer to emigrate to the U.S. I sit on the terrace of Venac while my aunt and another woman hang laundry. They tell me not to worry. The embassy will accept my application. So-and-so got in. So-and-so left. I am hopeful.

— my youngest sister and I crossing the border into Bosnia in a Yugo, heading to a place called Laktaši. Only now do I notice that Laktaši, when translated, means something like "elbow one's way in." Fitting. We take out the front seat, load a washing machine into the back, then put the seat back in for her to sit on. We strap two more to the roof and drive back to Serbia. A decent profit—300 DM, about $600 in today's money. After I move to America, my uncle keeps the scheme going. He tells me you can actually fit four washing machines in a Yugo—if you drive alone and leave the front seat at home.

— younger sister leaving on a double-decker bus with the English group, off to Paris to work as a nanny and learn French. She finds God, becomes a Christian, moves to the U.S. on a student visa. She never returns.

— Peter Handke visiting Venac. He hands out cash to kids and doesn't say who he is, but one refugee recognizes him from TV. He is an Austrian writer who would later win the Nobel Prize in Literature. We are sending our two smartest refugees to talk to him: the Teacher, who is eighteen, and a fellow refugee, seventeen, who would later become an artist living between Quito and Paris. Peter, impressed by the breadth of their knowledge, treats them to a fancy meal. He comes again the next day.

— a seventy-something man, a refugee at Venac like me, shuffling over, his stroke-weakened arm limp at his side. He holds out a nail clipper, asks if I'll cut his nails. I turn him away. A few days later, he jumps from the bathroom window and dies. I still think about it. I hate how weak she was.

— getting the news about our immigration application to the U.S. We have been rejected. I have the right to appeal. Sitting down and handwriting a five-page letter. I don't know if it will change anything. But I write anyway.

ACKNOWLEDGMENTS

Thanks to the editorial assessors, proofreaders, and designer who helped shape this book. They were paid—fairly—and the collaboration was clean, honest, and focused on the work itself, not the performance around it.

Thanks also to ChatGPT for assistance with editing, proofreading, and for generating the cover image of a man walking. I uploaded the manuscript, asked for an image that represents the work, and chose the first one it produced. It was good enough.

ABOUT THE AUTHOR

Sarah Majdov is a writer, technologist, and mother of two. She worked for years in the tech and finance sectors, where she witnessed how institutions reward illusion over substance. *Fatamorgana* is her first book—a meditation on what it takes to stop performing, what it costs to seek meaning honestly, and what becomes possible when we do.

Printed in Dunstable, United Kingdom

70567770R00208